The Romantic Tradition in American Literature

The Romantic Tradition in American Literature

Advisory Editor

HAROLD BLOOM
Professor of English, Yale University

ESSAYS AND POEMS

BY

JONES VERY

[R. W. EMERSON, editor]

ARNO PRESS

A NEW YORK TIMES COMPANY

New York • 1972

Reprint Edition 1972 by Arno Press Inc.

The Romantic Tradition in American Literature
ISBN for complete set: 0-405-04620-0
See last pages of this volume for titles.

Manufactured in the United States of America

಄ഌ಄ഌ಄ഌ಄ഌ಄ഌ಄ഌ಄ഌ಄ഌ

Library of Congress Cataloging in Publication Data

Very, Jones, 1813-1880.
    Essays and poems.

    (The Romantic tradition in American literature)
    Reprint of the 1839 ed.
    I. Title. II. Series.
PS3125.A2 1972   811'.3   72-4979
ISBN 0-405-04648-0

ESSAYS AND POEMS:

BY

JONES VERY.

———————

BOSTON:

CHARLES C. LITTLE AND JAMES BROWN.

———

MDCCCXXXIX.

Dutton & Wentworth, Print.

TO

EDWARD TYRREL CHANNING,

BOYLSTON PROFESSOR IN HARVARD UNIVERSITY,

THIS VOLUME IS INSCRIBED,

AS A TOKEN OF GRATITUDE,

BY THE AUTHOR.

CONTENTS.

═══

ESSAYS.

POEMS.

EPIC POETRY.

THE poets of the present day who would raise the epic song cry out, like Archimedes of old, "give us a place to stand on and we will move the world." This is, as we conceive, the true difficulty. Glancing for a moment at the progress of epic poetry, we shall see that the obscurity of fabulous times could be adapted to the earliest development only of the heroic character. There is an obvious incongruity in making times so far remote the theatre on which to represent the heroism of a civilized age; and it adds still more to the difficulty, that, although the darkness of fable still invests them, reason will no longer perceive the beings which the infant credulity of man once saw there.

To men in the early stages of society their physical existence must seem almost without end, and they live on through life with as little reference to

1

another state of being as we ourselves do in child-hood. To minds in this state there was a remoteness in an event which had taken place one or two centuries before, of which we cannot conceive, and which rendered the time that Homer had chosen for his subject, though not materially differing in charac-ter, sufficiently remote for his purpose. If to these advantages possessed by Homer we add those which belonged to him from the religion of his times and from tradition, whose voice is to the poet more friendly than the plain written records of history, we must confess that the spot on which he built up his scenes of heroic wonder was peculiarly favor-able. The advance, which the human mind had made towards civilization, prevented Virgil from making a like impression on his own age. To awaken admiration, he too was obliged to break from the bonds of the present, and soar beyond the bounds of history, before he could throw his spell of power over the mind. Why had he less influence ? Because he could not, like Homer, carry into the past the spirit of his times. To the enlarged minds of Virgil's day, the interval between the siege of Troy and their own time did not seem wider than it did to those who lived in the time of Homer. The true distance in time was chosen by each, but the character of Æneas did not possess those great attributes which could render it the Achilles of the

Romans. Lucan, while his characters exhibit the true heroic spirit of his age, fails of giving to them their due influence, from the want of some region of fiction beyond the dominion of history in which to place them. He cannot break from the present without violating every law of probability. To escape this thraldom and reach a point from which the heroic character of their age might be seen dilated to its full height, modern poets have fled beyond the bounds of time and woke the echoes of eternity. It was only from this point that the Christian world could be moved; it is only in that region without bounds, that the heroism of immortality can be shown in visible action. Milton and Dante chose this spot, on which with almost creative power they might show to mankind worlds of their own, " won from the void and formless Infinite," and from which their own heroic spirits might be reflected back upon their own times in all their gigantic proportions. But such has been the progress of the human mind since their time, that it would seem to have reached already another stage in its development, to have unfolded a new form of the heroic character, one which finds no paradise, nay, no heaven for itself in the creations of Milton, and for which the frowns of Dante's hell have no terror. This new page of the heroic character naturally leads us to inquire, whether we are to have no great representation of it, no embodying of this spirit in some gigantic form of action, which shall stalk before the age, and by the contemplation of which our minds may be fired to nobler deeds.

In considering this question, we shall endeavor to show what reasons there are for not expecting another great epic poem, drawn from the principles of epic poetry and the human mind, and that these present an insuperable barrier to the choice of a subject, which shall exhibit the present development of the heroic character in action.

In doing this I shall exhibit, by an analysis of the Iliad, the true model of an epic poem, its origin and peculiarities, and in what manner those peculiarities have been changed, and, at last, lost by succeeding poets, according to the development of the heroic character in their several eras.

I shall thus be led to show that the taking away of the peculiarities of *epic* interest, and the final emerging of that interest in the *dramatic*, is the natural result of the influences to which the human mind in its progress is subjected; and that that influence, while it precludes all former subjects from representing the present development of the heroic character, throws, at the same time, an insuperable barrier in the way of any subject.

Looking upon Homer, at least as regards the Iliad, as a single man speaking throughout with one accent

of voice, one form of language, and one expression
of feeling, we leave to the framers of modern para-
doxes the question, whether this name is a type or
not, and proceed to consider what might be the
probable origin of the Iliad, and what it is which
constitutes it the true model of an epic poem, a more
perfect visible manifestation of the heroic character
than can be again presented to the eyes of man.
In a philosophical analysis of such a poem as the
Iliad or Odyssey, made with reference to its epic
peculiarities, there is great danger of misconceiving
the history and character of early heroic poetry,
thus giving to the poet a plan which he never
formed, or a moral which he never conceiv-
ed. The simplest conception of the origin and
plan of the Iliad must, we think, prove the most
correct. It originated, doubtless, in that desire,
which every great poet must especially feel, of
revealing to his age forms of nobler beauty and
heroism than dwell in the minds of those around
him. Wandering, as his active imagination must
have led him to do, in the days of the past, Homer
must have been led by the fitness of the materials
presented to him in the siege of Troy, by their
remoteness from his own time, and the interest with
which they would be viewed by the mass of his
countrymen, as descendants of the Grecian heroes,
to the choice of a subject, which seemed to present

a worthy form in which to manifest the workings of
his soul. His enthusiasm would doubtless prompt
him to the execution of detached parts before he
had completed his general plan, and the various
incidents, which constitute so much of the charm
and interest of his poem as they suggested them-
selves to his mind, would also direct him to the great
point round which they all revolved. The influence
upon the several parts, resulting from the contem-
plation of the chief character, would thus give all
the unity to the subject which we find in fact to
belong to the earliest forms of a nation's poetry.
" Passion to excite sympathy, variety to prevent dis-
gust flowing in a free stream of narrative verse, not
the intricacy and dove-tailing of modern epics, is to
be looked for in the Iliad; for it was not made like
a modern epic to be read in our closets, but to be
presented only in fragments before the minds of an
audience. Thus the single combats of Menelaus
and Paris, the funeral games of Patroclus, and the
restitution and burial of the body of Hector are
generally complete in themselves, yet having an ob-
vious connexion as still telling the same great tale of
Troy." So much for the origin and fable of the Iliad.

The genius displayed in its grand and compre-
hensive design is only equalled by the judgment
manifested in confining the action to the busiest
and most interesting period of the Trojan war, in

thus uniting in his plan and bringing forward in his details everything which could lay hold of the affections, the prejudices, and vanity of his countrymen. Of his characters we need only say that, like those of Shakspeare, they are stamped with nature's own image and superscription. Though all are possessed of valor and courage, yet they are so distinguished from one another by certain peculiarities of disposition and manners, that to distinguish them it is hardly necessary to hear their names. Achilles is brave, and Hector is brave, so are Ajax, Menelaus, and Diomede ; but the bravery of Hector is not of the same kind with that of Ajax, and no one will mistake the battle-shout of the son of Atreus for the war-cry of Tydides.

Homer's machinery, as all epic machinery must be, was founded on the popular belief in the visible appearance of the gods ; and on account of this belief he was not less favored by the circumstances under which he introduced them, than he was by those which enabled him to represent his heroes. It cast around his whole subject a sublimity which it could not otherwise have had, giving occasion to noble description, and tending to excite that admiration which is the leading aim of the epic.

We have made this analysis of the Iliad, to show in what way all things combined in Homer's age to assist him in giving a perfect outward manifestation of the heroic character of his times. He wrote in that stage of society when man's physical existence assumed an importance in the mind, like that of our immortality, and gave to all without a power and dignity not their own. This it was which imparted an heroic greatness to war which cannot now be seen in it. That far-reaching idea of time, which seems to expand our thoughts with limitless existence, gives to our mental struggles a greatness they could not have before had. We each of us feel within our own bosoms a great, an immortal foe, which, if we have subdued, we may meet with calmness every other, knowing that earth contains no greater; but which, if we have not, it will continually appear in those petty contests with others by which we do but show our own cowardice. The Greeks, on the contrary, lived only for their country, and drew everything within the sphere of their national views; their highest exemplification of morality was patriotism. Of Homer's heroes it may with peculiar propriety be said that they were but children of a larger growth, and they could have no conception of power that was not perceived in its visible effects. "The world," as Milton says of our first parents, "was all *before* them," and not *within* them, and their mission was to go forth and make a material impression on the material world. The soul of Homer was the mirror of this outward world, and in his verse we have it shown to us with the distinctness and reality of the painter's page. Lucan calls him the prince of painters, and with him Cicero agrees, when he says, " Quæ species ac forma pugnæ, quæ acies, quod remigium, qui motus hominum, qui ferarum non ita expictus est, ut quæ ipse non viderit, nos ut videremus effecerit? " It is needless perhaps to say that this state of the mind gives both a reason and excuse for those many epithets, which a false criticism and a false delicacy of taste is so fond of censuring. Such critics would blame the poet for praising the physical strength of his heroes, in short for representing his gods such as they were believed to be, and painting his warriors such as they were. When we look back upon the pages of their history, we cannot contemplate the greatness there exhibited, without a feeling of sorrow that they had not lived under influences as favorable as our own, without a sense of unworthiness at not having exhibited characters corresponding with the high privileges we enjoy. We respect that grandeur of mind in the heroes of Homer which led them to sacrifice a mere earthly existence for the praise of all coming ages. They have not been disappointed. Worlds to them unknown have read of their deeds, and generations yet unborn shall honor them. They live on a page which the finger of time strives in vain to efface, which shall ever remain an eternal monument of

disgrace to those of after times, who, though gifted
with higher views of excellence, have yet striven to
erect a character on deeds like theirs. We rever-
ence not in Hector and Achilles the mere display of
physical power, we reverence not the manners of
their times which but too often call forth our horror
and disgust; but we do reverence and honor those
motives which even in the infancy of the human
mind served to raise it above the dominion of sense,
and taught it to grasp at a life beyond the narrow
limits of its earthly vision.

This state of things gave to the Iliad and Odyssey
that intense epic interest, which we fail to find in
later heroic poems. As the mind advances, a
stronger sympathy with the inner man of the heart
is more and more felt, and becomes more and more
the characteristic of literature. In the expanded
mind and cultivated affections, a new interest is
awakened, *dramatic* poetry succeds the *epic*, thus
satisfying the want produced by the farther devel-
opment of our nature. For the interest of the *epic*
consists in that character of greatness that in the
infancy of the mind is given to physical action and
the objects associated with it; but the interest of the
drama consists in those mental struggles which pre-
cede physical action, and to which in the progress
of man the greatness of the other becomes subor-
dinate. For as the mind expands and the moral

power is developed, the mightiest conflicts are born within, — outward actions lose their grandeur, except to the eye, for the soul looks upon them but as results of former battles won and lost, upon whose decision, and upon whose alone, its destiny hung. This is the mystery of that calm, more awful than the roar of battle, which rests on the spirits of the mighty, and which the hand of the Grecian sculptor strove to fix on the brow of his god. Though Homer has given variety to his poem by the introduction of dialogue, and thus rendered it, in one sense, often dramatic; yet we find it is the mere transferring of the *narrative* from his own lips to those of others. The interest is still *without*, it is not the interest of sentiment, but of description. This character of the Greeks, as might be supposed, is shown in their language; and illustrates their tendency in early times to look upon themselves in all reflex acts, whether external or internal, as patients rather than agents; a tendency to use the words of another, which is exemplified in every page of the Homeric poems, and which belongs more or less to every people in an early stage of civilization, before the nation comes of age, and acquires the consciousness along with the free use of its powers. This seems to be the reason why so many of the verbs employed by the Greeks to denote states of mind or of feeling, have a passive form, such as Φράζομαι,

Οἴομαι, Αἰσϑάνομαι, Σκέπτουαι, Ἐπίσταμαι, Βού-
λομαι, &c. "Men's minds," as Shakspeare has
somewhere said, "are parcel of their fortunes," and
his age was necessary and alone suited to the mind
of Homer. Man viewed himself with reference to
the world; not, as in the present day, the world in
reference to himself; and it was this state of the
mind which then made the taking of Troy the point
of epic interest.

We have thus endeavored to show that the mani-
festation of the heroic character in the time of
Homer was perfectly exhibited in outward visible
action, and that this reflected from the soul of the
poet addressed to a seeing and listening, rather than
a reading people, was the poetry of fancy rather
than sentiment. Events, characters, superstitions,
customs, and traditions, all combined in rendering
the Iliad a perfect embodying of the perfect outward
manifestation of the heroic character of that period.
The poetry of the senses, the reflection merely of
nature and of heroic achievements, is not suscepti-
ble of indefinite progress; it must evidently be most
perfect when the objects of visible action are noblest,
and we view all else only with reference to those
actions. The epic poetry of the Greeks corresponds
to sculpture, and in the one, as in the other, the
outward forms of life and action live and will ever
live unrivalled.

It is not our purpose to show the adaptation
of the rules of Aristotle to the Iliad, since from this
those rules were drawn, — we would only say that
according to the spirit of those rules every true epic
must be formed. They are not the arbitrary decis-
ions of a critic, but the voice of nature herself
speaking through her interpreter. Aristotle studied
nature in Homer; he gave no arbitrary rules, he
did but trace the pleasing effects produced on the
mind, and taught upon what those effects depended.
He may have erred in drawing his rules from one
development of the heroic character; but this was
the fault of his times, not of his judgment. He did
not mean that succeeding poets should bow to him,
but should reverence those great principles to which
he had shown that nature herself had conformed in
her noblest work. The true poet will look without
for no rules drawn from others; he feels within
himself the living standard of the great and beau-
tiful, and bows to that alone: as far as it has become
changed by human error or imperfection, he would
gladly restore it to its original purity, by a conform-
ity to those universal laws of sublimity and beauty,
which the critic has shown to be followed by nature
herself.

When Aristotle tells us that the action of an epic
should be one and entire, and that it should be a
great action, he tells us of what constitutes its

essence, and of that without which it ceases to be such a poem. It must be one and entire that the interest may not be distracted, and that the mind may feel the harmony of all its proportions. It is not the poet of fancy who can bind by his spell the parts of such a fabric, it is the poet who has felt more strongly than any other the great moral wants of his age, that can give to such a work its unity and power. It has been well said that in reading the gay creations of Ariosto, — of his fairy bowers and castles and palaces, — we are for a moment charmed and wrapt in pleasant reveries, but they are but dreams; the impression is soon shaken off; we are conscious of no master-feeling round which they gather, and which alone could render his poem an epic, the noblest of harmonious creations. But in reading the Iliad, or a tragedy like Lear or Macbeth, or in looking sometime at a painting on which the moral sentiment of the artist is as strongly impressed as his imagination, instead of being obliged to humor the fancy that the charm may be kept alive, we shall with difficulty shake off the impression, when it is necessary to return to the real business of life. It is in the greatness of the epic action that the poets succeeding Homer, if we except Milton have failed; and the causes which have operated against them, will always operate with increasing force against every attempt to represent the present or future development of the heroic character in action. It is in the childhood of the human mind alone, that the interval between thought and action is the widest, and therefore it is then alone that the events occupying that interval can be best described. The great struggle of the epic poets since the time of Homer has been against this narrowing of their field of action, and making the instruments there employed less visible, less tangible. The wonder and interest of the world is now transferred to the mind, whose thought is action, and whose word is power. Lord Kames therefore erred, when he said "that it was the *familiarity* of modern manners that unqualified them for epic poetry, and that the dignity of present manners would be better understood in future ages, when they are no longer familiar." The fact is, our manners, or the manners and actions of any intellectual nation, can never become the representatives of greatness, — they have fallen from the high sphere which they occupied in a less advanced stage of the human mind, never to regain it. This will account for the appearance among us of such works as the " Sartor Resartus," whose object is to impress the forms of physical life with a greatness no longer belonging to them, and which we recognise only in spiritual action.

These remarks will show why it was that Virgil failed in making the same impression on his age, that was made by his great model. His poem is but a lunar reflection of the Iliad; and it was perhaps from a deep consciousness of this, that he ordered it in his will to be burned. That poem, which was the natural expression of the early features of society, could only be faintly copied by the mimic hand of art. Virgil's subject is well chosen, and would not have shone with reflected light had it been treated of in the early days of Rome. He summoned again from their long sleep the heroes and gods of Troy, but they appeared with dimmed glory amid the brightness of another age. He had, as we have before observed, chosen the right point in time for his action, a time of tradition, affording him all the advantages possessed by Homer, but not to transgress the laws of probability, he could not give his hero the character of another age, he could not make Æneas the Achilles of the Romans. Virgil as well as Lucan has been blamed by the critics; the one, for not giving to his hero the dignity of thought becoming the heroic character of his own time; the other, for not placing his action beyond the strict bounds of history. In regard to each we think the critics have erred; for neither the time nor the characters could have been changed without producing a strange incongruity.

Thus the epic poets of Greece and Rome, who succeeded Homer, must have labored under peculiar

disadvantages to which those of modern times are
are not subjected. If, like Virgil, they had chosen
the same time for their action with Homer, they
could not transfer to it the heroic spirit of their own
day, at least, in its noblest development, — they
could not make a Cato or a Brutus cotemporary with
an Achilles or an Ajax; — they must evoke the
heroic spirits of other days, spirits reluctant to obey
the spells employed by the magicians of another
age. Virgil, as well as every other poet whose
action lies in times very far distant from his own,
has not the greatest difficulty to overcome, in exhib-
iting characters moved by those same affections and
sympathies which unite the ceaseless generations of
men, in giving to the slumbering past the emotions
of the present; but in *adapting* to the story of a
former age, and perhaps foreign nation, that peculiar
system of manners which constitutes the outward
development of the heroic spirit, and of which no
mind, but such as has been subjected to its actual
influence, can either strongly feel or vividly describe.
These manners perish with their age, — there is no
hand of enchantment to wave over them and convert
them, like the fabled city of Arabian romance, into
living stone; no convulsion of nature, like that
which covered* Pompeii, to wrap them in a veil
which future ages might withdraw, and permit them,
untouched by the hand of time, to stand unimpaired

2

amid the ruins of the past, and gaze with wonder on the new-risen generations of men. But if, like Lucan, they took their subject from the hands of History, the skepticism of a more advanced age deprived them of the use of machinery, and consequently of the power of exciting that admiration, which is the leading aim of the epic poem. We need not stop to show how ridiculous Iris would have appeared on the plains of Pharsalia bringing a sword to Pompey, or Venus coming to snatch him away in a cloud. It is evident that the poet, forced to follow in the same path with the historian, must feel the bonds of reality continually restraining and checking his native energies.

These difficulties the influence of Christianity overcame, but subjected the epic poet to others still more discouraging, as I shall endeavor to show by a brief reference to Tasso, Dante, and Milton.

The subject chosen by Tasso, and the time of the action of his poem, bore the same relation to Christian civilization as Homer's did to Grecian. It was the only age in which the heroic Christian character could be fully manifested in outward action. This resulted from a peculiar state of the mind which, as we have said in regard to heroic manners, perishes with its age, with the circumstances that called it forth. It was a new development of the Homeric spirit modified by Christianity. The interest as in the Iliad and Æneid is all *without*, and this it is which gives to the poem of Tasso, as to the other two, the true epic interest, and adds a dignity to the manners of these poems belonging to no other, where the subject is taken from the common events of life. The subject, too, as it presented a scene for the display of action resulting from a purer faith, possesses a dignity far surpassing that of his two great predecessors. Thus fortunate in his subject and in the time of his action, he was equally favored by the popular belief of his age. By the superstition of his own time he was enabled to oppose with success the light of reality which was thrown around his subject by history, and give to it that supernatural interest, which is found so capable of exciting admiration. However, in our cooler moments, we may laugh at his magicians and their incantations, as they are not mere embodied abstractions, like Voltaire's agents, but founded on the actual belief of his day, they will always possess a reality to the mind ; and, when in reading we have yielded for a time to our feelings, will again assert their power. We have placed Tasso before Dante, in order of time, because he has given an earlier development of the heroic character. He would, doubtless, have possessed as well as Virgil, whom he has so closely followed, greater originality, and more strongly exhibited that development, had he lived nearer the age he endeavored to portray.

The effect of Christianity was to make the individual mind the great object of regard, the centre of eternal interest, and transferring the scene of action from the outward world to the world within, to give to all modern literature the dramatic tendency, — and as the mind of Homer led him to sing of the physical conflicts of his heroes with *visible* gods *without;* so the soul of the modern poet, feeling itself contending with motives of godlike power *within*, must express that conflict in the dramatic form, in the poetry of sentiment. Were the present a fit opportunity, Shakspeare might afford us still farther illustrations of this truth, and especially in the character of Hamlet, of whom a critic has truly said, "we love him not, we think of him not, because he is witty, because he was melancholy, because he was filial; but we love him because he existed, and was himself. This is the sum total of the impression. I believe that of every other character, either in tragic or epic poetry, the story makes part of the conception; but of Hamlet the deep and permanent interest is the conception of himself. This seems to belong not to the character being more perfectly drawn, but to there being a more intense conception of individual human life, than perhaps in any other human composition."

The Sartor Resartus, Lamartine's Pilgrimage, Words-
worth's poem on the Growth of an Individual Mind,
all obey the same law, — which is, that as Chris-
tianity influences us, we shall lay open to the world
what has been long hidden, what has before been
done in the secret corners of our own bosoms ; the
knowledge of which can alone make our intercourse
with those about us different from what it is too fast
becoming, an intercourse of the eye and the ear and
the hand and the tongue. This may serve to reveal
to us more clearly the principle which led to the
selection of the subjects of all the great epic poems
of modern times ; for it was only by making man
the subject, around which might be gathered the
material forms of grandeur and beauty, that an
interest could be imparted to the epic corresponding
to that of the drama. The poem of Tasso forms
the only exception to this remark, and this, as we
have shown, does but confirm our observation ; for
it represents the mind essentially pagan, yet moved
by Christianity, and finding, like the Greek, all its
motive for action without. Our interest in the poem
is consequently much less than in those which ex-
hibit the later developments of the Christian heroic
character.

By removing the bounds of time, Christianity has,
I think, rendered every finite subject unsuited for an
epic poem. The Christian creed, in opening the

vista of eternity before the poet's view, and leaving
him unrestrained by prescriptive forms, while it
freed him from the bonds of history, by giving him
a place beyond its limits where he might transfer
the heroic spirit of his age, and surround his heroes
with supernatural agents, capable of raising for his
action the highest admiration, subjected him to a far
greater difficulty than any yet experienced by former
poets ; that of finding a subject, an action to fill
those boundless realms of space, and call forth the
energies of the spirits that people it. In considering
the efforts which Christian poets have made to over-
come this difficulty, and bridge the space between
time and eternity, we shall find the great reason for
not expecting another attempt, so successful as that
made by Milton, arising from circumstances which
have rendered the difficulty far more formidable
since his time.

If we consider Tasso as having chosen a subject
exhibiting the first development of the Christian
heroic character, the poem of Dante will exhibit to
us the second. Though not an epic, if viewed with
reference to classical models whose aim and spirit
were intrinsically different from any produced since,
it will serve to show how the genius of Dante over-
came the difficulty we have mentioned. His poem
is unique, but produced under circumstances which
would have rendered it, if the obstacles we have

alluded to had not opposed, a regular epic poem. It had its origin, like other sublime works of genius, in that desire, which is continually felt by the greatest minds, of giving to their age a copy of their own souls, and embodied the vague but universal spirit of the times when it was written. Its foundations were the popular creed of all Christendom; its supports, the deep reasonings and curious subtilties of countless theologians; and the scenes it represents, such as had long formed the dreams of many a monk on Vallombrosa, and perhaps entered into the sermon of every preacher in Europe.

Thus, although the circumstances which gave birth to Dante's poem, were, if we may so say, epic, yet the form which that poem took, shows the hostility which the Christian influence has towards the strictly classical model. That influence had already divested of its greatness every subject like that of Homer's or Virgil's, and turned upon himself, as an individual, the interest which man in their times had given to the outward world. It is in Dante's poem that we find man, as a physical being, first made the great point of epic interest. He is the first epic poet that exhibits the tendency we have so often alluded to. Favored beyond succeeding poets by the belief of his age, he was enabled to gather around man beings which his ignorance and fear shrouded in a sublimity not their own. That

strange world of beings, which the spirit creates for
itself, has fled before the light of science ; their
forms no longer float in the fairy halls of earth, nor
throng the untravelled regions of space. Their
foot-prints, which our infant eyes saw impressed on
this strange world of ours, and which once conjured
up so many and wondrous shapes of beauty or
terròr, tell us now but of one creative spirit in whom
we recognise our Father.

> " The intelligible forms of ancient poets,
> The fair humanities of old religion,
> The power, the beauty, and the majesty
> That had their haunts in dale, or piny mountain,
> Or forest by slow stream, or pebbly spring,
> Or chasms or watery depths, — all these have
>   vanished.;
> They live no longer in the faith of reason."

In Dante's time, Hell, Purgatory, and Heaven
had long been considered as the separate states in
which vice and virtue would meet their fitting re-
ward. This belief had been taught by signs and
emblems ; and those of his day had been made to
learn rather through the medium of their senses,
than the silent arguments of conscience " accusing
or excusing itself," what were the rewards and
punishments of the future world. This material

development of Christianity it was Dante's mission to hold up to his age, and upon that age it must have had and did have its greatest influence; for it was produced by the power of materiality which is lessened with every advance of the Christian character. His poem plainly shows that the tendency which Christianity gave to poetry was not to the epic but to the dramatic form, and if it freed the heroic poet from difficulties to which he was before liable, it also exposed him to another, which, although evaded by Milton, must in the end prove fatal.

The next and highest development of the heroic character, yet shown in action, was that exhibited by the sublime genius of Milton. The mind had taken a flight above the materiality of Dante, and resting between that and the pure spirituality of the present day, afforded him a foundation for his action. He could not adopt altogether the material or the immaterial system, and he therefore raised his structure on the then debatable ground. The greatest objection, which our minds urge against his agents, is the incongruity between their spiritual properties and the human modes of existence, he was obliged to ascribe to them. But this is an objection of our own times, of men requiring a more spiritual representation of the mind's action, which, if it cannot be given, must preclude the possibility of another great epic. In fact, Milton's poem but confirms more strongly the conclusion we drew from Dante's, that *dramatic* is supplying the place of epic interest. His long deliberation in the choice of a subject suited to his conceptions, shows the *difficulty then* lying in the way of an epic; and his first intention of making Paradise Lost a *tragedy*, shows *whence* this difficulty originated. The tendency of the mind, to which we have before alluded, and which had grown yet stronger in Milton's time than before, compelled him to make choice of the *Fall of Man* as his subject; a subject exclusive in its nature, being the only one which to our minds possesses a great epic interest. The interest of his poem depends upon the strong feeling we have of our own free agency, and of the almost infinite power it is capable of exercising. An intense feeling of this kind seems to have pervaded Milton's whole life, and by this he was probably directed in the choice of his theme. We find in his " Speech for the Liberty of unlicensed Printing," written many years before the conception of his poem, a sentence confirming this supposition. " Many," says he, " there be that complain of Divine Providence for suffering Adam to transgress. Foolish tongues ! When God gave him reason, he gave him freedom to choose; for reason is but choosing. He had been else a mere artificial Adam, such an Adam as he is in the motions. We ourselves esteem not of that

obedience or love or gift which is of force." This
feeling becomes stronger the more the mind is influ-
enced by Christianity, and this it is which has trans-
ferred the interest from the outward manifestation of
the passions exhibited in the Iliad, to those inward
struggles made by a power greater than they to
control them, and cause them, instead of bursting
forth like lava-torrents to devour and blast the face
of nature, to flow on like meadow-streams of life
and joy. Why then it may be asked do we take an
interest in Homer's heroes, whom the gods are ready
every moment to shield or snatch from the dubious
fight? Not, I answer, because we consider them
mere machines acting but from others' impulses, for
then we could take no interest in them; but because
when

> " Arms on armor clashing bray
> Horrible discord, and the madding wheels
> Of brazen chariots rage,"

we give to them our own freedom; or because the
gods themselves, whom Homer has called down to
swell the fight, and embodied in his heroes; because
these create the interest and make what were before
mere puppets free agents. When, in our cooler
moments, we reflect on his Jove-protected warriors,
his invulnerable Achilles, — they dwindle into insig-
nificance, and we are ready to exclaim in the quaint

language of another, "Bully Dawson would have fought the devil with such advantages."

This sense of free agency is what constitutes Adam the hero of Paradise Lost, and makes him capable of sustaining the immense weight of interest, which in this poem is made to rest upon him. But that which renders Adam the hero of the poem, makes Satan still more so; for Milton has opened to our gaze, within his breast of flame, passions of almost infinite growth, burning with intensest rage. *There* is seen a conflict of "those thoughts that wander through eternity," at the sight of which we lose all sense of the material terrors of that fiery hell around him, and compared with which the physical conflict of the archangels is a mockery. It is not so much that battles present less a subject for description than they did in the time of Homer, that they fail to awaken those feelings of admiration they then did, but because we have become sensible of a power within which bids the tide of war roll back upon its fountains. For the same reason it is that the *manners* of civilized nations are unsuited for heroic song. They are no longer the representatives of greatness; for the heroism of Christianity is not seen so much in the outward act, as in the struggle of the will to control the springs of action. It is this which gives to tragedy its superiority over the epic at the present day; it strikes off the chains

of wonder by which man has been so long fettered
to the objects of sense, and, instead of calling upon
him to admire the torrent-streams of war, it bids
the bosom open whence they rushed, and points him
downward to their source, the ocean might of the
soul,

> " Dark — heaving — boundless, endless, and sub-
>   lime —
> The image of eternity — the throne
> Of the Invisible."

Thus Milton's poem is the most favorable model
we can have of a Christian epic. The subject of it
afforded him the only field of great epic interest,
where the greatest power could be shown engaged
in bringing about the greatest results. Adam is not
so much the Achilles as the Troy of the poem.
And there is no better proof that greatness has left
the material throne, which she has so long held, for
a spiritual one, than that Milton, in putting in motion
that vast machinery which he did to effect his pur-
pose, seems as if he made, like Ptolemy, the sun
and all the innumerable hosts of heaven again to
revolve about this little spot of earth. Though he
has not made the Fall of Man a tragedy in *form*,
as he first designed, he has yet made it tragic in
spirit; and the epic form it has taken seems but the

drapery of another interest.   This proves that, how-
ever favored by his subject, the epic poet of our day
may be, he must by the laws of his own being
possess an introspective mind, and give that which
Bacon calls an inwardness of meaning to his char-
acters, which, in proportion as the mind advances,
must diminish that greatness once shown in visible
action.   The Christian Knights might well exclaim,
when they first saw gunpowder used in war, as
Plutarch tells us the king of Sparta did, when he
saw a machine for the casting of stones and darts,
that it was " the grave of valor."   They were the
graves of that personal valor which is shown in
its perfection in the infancy of the mind, and which
is imaged in the pages of Homer.   In modern bat-
tles, the individuality of early times is lost and
merged in one great head, with reference to which
we view all results.   The men upon whom the
superior mind acts are mere mechanical instruments
of its power, and the deeds seen by the outward
eye are thus dimmed by the soul's quicker perception
of spiritual action.   Thus the intellectual power
wielded by the commander seems already to have
decided the battle, and we look with less interest upon
his army's incursions into the territory of an enemy.
As Sallust says of Jugurtha, " totum regnum animo
jam invaserat."

     To complain of this tendency of the human mind

and its influence on literature, to sigh that we cannot have another Homeric poem, is like weeping for the feeble days of childhood, and shows an insensibility to the ever-increasing beauty and grandeur developed by the spirit in its endless progress, a forgetfulness of those powers of soul which result from this very progress, which enable it, while enjoying the present, to add to that joy by the remembrance of the past, and to grasp at a higher from the anticipations of the future. With the progress of the arts, power is manifested by an agency almost as invisible as itself; it almost speaks and it is done, it almost commands and it stands fast. Man needs no longer a vast array of physical means to effect his loftiest purpose ; he seizes the quill, the mere toy of a child, and stamps on the glowing page the copy of his own mind, his thoughts pregnant with celestial fire, and sends them forth, wherever the winds of heaven blow or its light penetrates, the winged messengers of his pleasure. The narrow walls of patriotism are broken down, and he is a brother on whom the same sun shines, and who holds the same heritage, the earth. He is learning to reverse the order in which the ancients looked at the outward creation, he looks at the world with reference to himself, and not at himself with reference to the world. How different the view which Virgil takes

of his country from that of the Christian poet; yet
each how worthy of its age!

" Sed neque Medorum silvæ, ditissima terra,
   Nec pulcher Ganges, atque auro turbidus Hermus,
   Laudibus Italiæ certent; non Bactra, neque Indi,
   Totaque thuriferis Panchaia pinguis arenis.
   Hæc loca non tauri spirantes naribus ignem
   Invertêre, satis immanis dentibus hydri;
   Nec galeis densisque virûm seges horruit hastis:
   Sed gravidæ fruges et Bacchi Massicus humor
   Implevêre; tenent oleæ, armentaque loeta.
   Hinc bellator equus campo sese arduus infert;
   Hinc albi, Clitumne, greges, et maxima taurus
   Victima, sœpe tuo perfusi flumine sacro,
   Romanos ad templa deûm duxêre triumphos.
   Hîc ver assiduum, atque alienis mensibus æstas;
   Bis gravidæ pecudes, bis pomis utilis arbor."

                    " O my mother isle!
Needs must thou prove a name most dear and holy
To me, a son, a brother, and a friend,
A husband, and a father! who revere
All bonds of natural love, and find them all
Within the limits of thy rocky shores.
O native Britain! O my mother isle!
How shouldst thou prove aught else but dear and
      holy

To me, who from thy lakes, and mountain-hills,
Thy clouds, thy quiet dales, thy rocks, and seas
Have drunk in all my intellectual life,
All sweet sensations, all ennobling thoughts,
All adoration of the God in nature,
All lovely and all honorable things,
Whatever makes this mortal spirit feel
The joy and greatness of its future being?"

We cannot sympathize with that spirit of criticism, which censures modern poetry for being the portraiture of individual characteristics and passions, and not the reflection of the general features of society and the outward man. If we want such poetry as Homer's, we must not only evoke him from the shades, but also his times. Purely objective poetry is the most perfect, and possesses the most interest, only in the childhood of the human mind. In the poetry of the Hindoos, of the Israelites, as well as of the Greeks, the epic is the prevailing element. But that page of the heroic character is turned forever; — another element is developing itself in the soul, and breathing into the materiality of the past a spiritual life and beauty. It is in vain we echo the words of other days, and call it poetry; it is in vain we collect the scattered dust of the past, and attempt to give it form and life by that same principle which once animated it. We can only

3

give a brighter and more joyous existence to the
cold forms of departed days, by bowing down, like
the prophet of old, and breathing into them a purer
and more ennobling faith, the brighter flame of our
own bosoms. To stir the secret depths of our
hearts, writers must have penetrated deeply into
their own. Homer found conflicts *without*, to de-
scribe; shall the poets of our day be blamed because
they would exhibit to us those they feel *within*?
Milton gives us the philosophy of Christian epic
poets, when he says, " that he who would not be
frustrate of his hope to write well hereafter in lauda-
ble things, ought himself to be a true poem; that is,
a composition and pattern of the best and honorablest
things; not presuming to sing of high praises of
heroic men or famous cities, unless he have in him-
self the experience and practice of all that which is
praiseworthy." What, indeed, are the writings of
the great poets of our own times but epics; the
description of those internal conflicts, the interest in
which has so far superseded those of the outward
world? A sufficient answer to the charge of ego-
tism and selfishness, to which they are exposed, is
given in the words of Coleridge. " In the Paradise
Lost, indeed in every one of his poems, it is Milton
himself whom you see; his Satan, his Adam, his
Raphael, almost his Eve, are all John Milton; and
it is a sense of this intense egotism that gives me

the greatest pleasure in reading Milton's works.
The egotism of such a man is a revelation of spirit."
Lamartine, when he complains so often at not being
able to give to the world an epic embodying the
present development of the heroic character, seems
not to have dreamed that, unless he could represent
objectively the action of one mind on another, he
was, by the expression of his feelings, giving us the
only epic poem the mind in its present stage is capa-
ble of giving.

The truth of the principles, we have laid down,
may be still farther tested by their application to
the projected epic of Coleridge on the destruction
of Jerusalem, of which he said that it " was the
only subject now remaining for an epic poem, a
subject which, like Milton's Fall of Man, should
interest all Christendom, as the Homeric war of
Troy interested all Greece." He farther observes,
that " the subject with all its great capabilities has
this one grand defect, that whereas a poem to be
epic must have a *personal* interest in the destruction
of Jerusalem, no genius or skill could possibly pre-
serve the interest for the hero from being merged in
the interest for the event." We will not touch upon
other objections which he himself has urged, such
as mythology and manners, to which what we have
already said on other poems, will as well apply;
but will only remark, that the subject itself is incapa-

ble of exhibiting the present development of the
heroic character, and cannot therefore be made the
great epic of this age, or of any to come. This
may be seen from what has already been said. What
made Milton's subject great, and what can *now*
alone make any subject for epic interest great, was
the action made *visible* of a superior intellect on an
inferior. Could intellectual power be represented
with the same objectiveness as physical power, there
might be as many epics now as there are great
minds. The reason is obvious. It is this manner
of representing power which alone possesses a cor-
responding interest with tragedy, by which alone
there can be a *hero* capable of sustaining the inter-
est. The poem of Coleridge, even if feasible, must
have been more similar to Tasso's than Milton's, and
consequently when compared with the latter, not
great.

Schiller's plan of an epic poem, founded on Fred-
erick the Great of Prussia as the hero, must, if the
principles advanced are correct, have proved far
more futile than the one last mentioned; and it
strongly confirms, as we think, the remarks before
made on the hostility of the dramatic to the epic
interest, that two of the greatest poets of our age
should each have schemed an epic, yet neither com-
pleted one.

Of such attempts at the epic, as Monti's in Italian,

and Pollok's in our own language, we will only say, that they are as much wanting in the spirit of an epic as in its true form, and that they are as remote from the merit of Dante, whom they have taken as their model, as near him in plan. Their poems resemble those Spanish epics which suddenly appeared in the reign of Philip the Second, the whole series of which were nothing but chronicles, and differed but little from histories. Of Wilkie, and a host of others, we might say as Giraldi Cinto said of Trissino, who employed twenty years on his "Italia Liberata," that they do but select the refuse from the gold of Homer, imitate his vices, and gather together all that which good judges would wish to be rid of, by which they show little wisdom.

We have thus endeavored to show the inability of the human mind, at the present day, to represent objectively its own action on another mind, and that the power to do this could alone enable the poet to embody in his hero the present development of the heroic character, and give to his poem a universal interest. We rejoice at this inability; it is the high privilege of our age, the greatest proof of the progress of the soul, and of its approach to that state of being where its thought is action, its word power.

SHAKSPEARE.

It is pleasing to frequent the places from which the feet of those whom this world calls great have passed away, to see the same groves and streams that they saw, to hear the same sabbath bells, to linger beneath the roof under which they lived, and be shaded by the same tree which shaded them. It is pleasant, for it makes us, as it were, companions of their earthly presence ; — the same heaven is above us, and the same earth is beneath us, and we feel ourselves sharers, for a time, in the same earthly heritage. But for the soul this is not enough. We feel unsatisfied until we know ourselves akin even with that greatness which made the spots on which it rested hallowed ; and until, by our own lives, and by converse with the thoughts they have bequeathed us, we feel that union and relationship of the spirit which we seek. We may frequent the same shades, we may linger beside the same streams, the mind may be raised and improved by its intercourse with a superior mind, but we can never be at rest, at home with them, we can never really see the same heaven and the same earth, either that our fellow men or that the Father of our spirits beholds, until by our own life that perfect union and relationship has been consummated.   With other writers, at our very first acquaintance with their thoughts, we recognise our relationship with the swiftness of intuition ; but who of us, however familiar he may have been with his writings, has yet caught a glance of Shakspeare's self, so that he could in any way identify himself with him, and feel himself a sharer in his joys and sorrows, his motives and his life ?   With views narrowed down to our own peculiar and selfish ends, we cannot well conceive, for we feel little within us that answers to a being like him — whose spirit seemed the antagonist of matter ; whose life was as various and all-embracing as nature's ; and in whom the individual seemed lost and blended with the universal.   In him we have a gift not of a world of matter but one of mind ; — a spirit to whom time and place seemed not to adhere ; to whom all seasons were congenial ; the world a home ; who was related to us all in that which is most ourselves ; and whose life and character, the more we lay aside what in us is provincial and selfish, the more deeply shall we understand. In speaking of him and what he did as an exception to ordinary rules, we only confess our ignorance of the great law of his existence. If he was natural, and by a common nature kindred with us, as we all confess, that ignorance, which only exists by our own sufferance, will clear up, as we lay aside all that is false and artificial in our characters, and Shakspeare and his creations will stand before us in the clear bright sun-light of our own consciousness.

My object is to show, by an analysis of the character of Shakspeare, that a desire of action was the ruling impulse of his mind; and consequently a sense of existence its permanent state. That this condition was natural; not the result felt from a submission of the will to it, but bearing the will along with it; presenting the mind as phenomenal and unconscious, and almost as much a passive instrument as the material world.

I shall thus be led to find excuse for much that has seemed impure in his writings, and to change that admiration which has hitherto regarded him as a man, into one which would look upon him and love him as the unconscious work of God.

By doing this I shall show that there is a higher action than that we witness in him; where the will has not been borne down and drawn along by the mind's own original impulse; but, though capable

of resistance, yields flexibly to all its natural move-
ments, presenting that higher phenomenon which
genius and revelation were meant to forward in all
men, — conscious nature.

Our view is not concerned, therefore, with those
necessary motives which doubtless compelled Shaks-
peare, like all of us, to provide a daily means of
support. These are matters of external history.
They are indeed prominent objects, often changing
and giving a new direction to the current; but they
tell us not why it flows onward and will ever flow.
It is not to the softer and more perishable parts of
his massy mind, I would direct my attention; but to
those veins of a primitive formation, which, now that
time has loosened and removed all else, still stand
out as the iron frame work of his being. We look
upon such minds as Shakspeare's as exceptions, for
wise purposes, to our common nature; and as the
single man who is born blind tells thousands that
there is One who giveth them sight; so those of our
race, who by nature are so strongly prompted to will
and to do that their minds seem almost as passive as
matter beneath superior power, have been denied
the liberty of will, as I think, that the many might
be continually reminded that their minds were not
their own, and that the conscious submission of their
wills to the same great influence was their highest
glory. All men will then exhibit, according to their

gifts, that greatness and universality as conscious, which we now witness in them unconsciously shown; their ruling motive will be a yielding to the hallowed impulses to action; — the permanent state of their souls, eternal life.

There is a desire of mental activity felt by such a mind as Shakspeare's corresponding with that impulse to physical action felt by all men. This must be a natural consequence of such mental endowment; and the movements of the mind, in men like these, must as regularly take the lead of volition as the involuntary motions of the physical frame. Scott's confession on this point applies equally to all. "People may say this and that of the pleasure of fame or of profit as a motive of writing: I think the *only* pleasure is in the actual exertion and research, and I would no more write upon any other terms than I would hunt merely to dine upon hare-soup.' At the same time, if credit and profit came unlooked for, I would no more quarrel with them than with the soup." The main action of all such minds must evidently be as independent of the will as is the life in a plant or a tree; and, as they are but different results of the same great vital energy in nature, we cannot but feel that the works of genius are as much a *growth* as are the productions of the material world. Such minds act as if all else but the sense of their existence was an accident; and, under the

influence of this transforming power, all is plastic ; —
marble becomes flexible and shapes itself into life ;
words partake as it were of motion, form and speech ;
and matter, like the atoms on the magnetic plate,
feels instinct with order and design.   The stream of
life, — which, in other men, obstructed and at last sta-
tionary as the objects that surround it, seems scarcely
to deserve the name, — in them rolls ever onward its
rich and life-giving waters as if unconscious of the
beautiful banks it has overflowed with fertility. With
most men it requires a continual effort of the will
to prevent the objects which were only intended to
give exercise to their souls from detaining them, as
it were, and holding them in a torpid inanimation.
As long as man labors for a physical existence,
though an act of necessity almost, he is yet natural ;
it is life, though that of this world, for which he
instinctively works.   But when he has reached this
point where the means of physical existence are se-
cured, he is permitted to become unnatural ; he is
left at liberty to strive for that eternal life which is
promised him, by the voluntary surrender and sacri-
fice of the objects of this ; or to become at every
moment more like the senseless clods around him,
and, at last, when he has gained the whole world,
instead of having sacrificed it all to that sense of
life and love within him, he has lost his soul.   It
seems indeed a thing impossible to us, sunk as we are

in sin and the flesh, that this vast globe and millions of others should roll on their limitless ways with the speed of thought, moved but by a will kindred with our own. But would we take our just position in regard to the objects of sense; and, instead of finding ourselves revolving around them, did they seem like harmonized spheres enlightened and moved by the strong working principles of duty and love within us, we should then indeed feel of a truth our relationship to our Father, and that for matter to obey His will was but its natural law. Do we wonder then, that, as this momentary petrifaction of the heart goes on, we are every day more and more strangers in this world of love, holding no communion with the Universal Parent, and hoarding up instead of distributing His general gifts? As we resist this process, the resulting state must evidently be one with which we may interpret the mind of Shakspeare,—a sense of eternal life, an activity communicated to all else, and not merely one communicated to us from without; we are no longer the servants of sin, but the free followers of Christ.

As, therefore, the activity of the mind, freed by an exertion of the will, must ever be connected with the sense of eternal life, so is there joined with the mind's involuntary freedom a sense of existence that constitutes its innocent happiness, and makes it the natural teacher to us of the wide principle which is its mission. In Claudio's reflections on death, the poet unconsciously lays bare the texture of his own mind. Claudio regrets not, as we should suppose he would, the loss of his sister, or the good things of this world, nor feels a doubt of another; but all his horrors are but the negations of these two great characteristics of Shakspeare's own mind, — the barring up of his varied activity, and the losing in a kneaded clod of the sensible warm motion of life.

> " Ay, but to die, and go we know not where;
>   To lie in cold obstruction, and to rot;
>   This sensible warm motion to become
>   A kneaded clod; and the delighted spirit
>   To bathe in fiery floods, or to reside
>   In thrilling regions of thick-ribbed ice;
>   To be imprisoned in the viewless winds,
>   And blown with restless violence round about
>   The pendent world; or to be worse than worst
>   Of those that lawless and uncertain thoughts
>   Imagine howling! — 'tis too horrible!
>   The weariest and most loathed worldly life,
>   That age, ache, penury, and imprisonment
>   Can lay on nature, is a paradise
>   To what we fear of death."

And again, in Clarence's dream of death, so strongly is the resistance of the soul to this imprisoning of it

expressed, that˙ we feel a sense of suffocation in
reading it.

> "Often did I strive
> To yield the ghost: but still the envious flood
> Kept in my soul, and would not let it forth
> To seek the empty, vast, and wand'ring air;
> But smother'd it within my panting bulk,
> Which almost burst to belch it in the sea."

The play of Hamlet is founded on these two char-
acteristics, and they are apparent throughout; as we
shall endeavor to show by a separate analysis of it.
We are continually hearing the poet himself speak-
ing out through the words of Hamlet. As we be-
come more and more conscious of that state of mind
which our Savior calls eternal life, we shall the bet-
ter understand the natural superiority of such a mind
as Shakspeare's to the narrowing influences which
we have to resist, but which his involuntary activity
rendered powerless. That a sense of life would be
the accompaniment of this activity would then be
apparent; for how could that childlike love of vari-
ety and joyous sympathy with all things exist, save
from that simple happiness which in him ever flowed
from the consciousness of being, but which, alas, by
most of us is known but in youth? Between the
dignified and trivial, between decay and bloom, how
else could he have felt that connecting link, of which

we are insensible, enabling him to present them all
united as in the moving panorama that encircles us.
This life of his in all objects and scenes was the
simple result of the movements of a mind which
found only in all it saw around it, something to cor-
respond with its own condition. Its own activity was
its possession; circumstances and things seemed to
be, because it was; these were accidents, and not, as
with other men, realities. His power while exerted
on every thing seems independent of its objects.
Like the ocean, his mind could fill with murmuring
waves the strangely indented coast of human exist-
ence from the widest bay to the smallest creek; then
ebbing, retire within itself, as if form was but a mode
of its limitless and independent being. Did love
succeed necessity, we should need no other explana-
tion of such a mind than our own would give us.
We all feel at first that the life is more than the
meat, but from the corrupt world around us we soon
learn to prize the meat more than our spiritual life.
We learn indeed, while children, the fallacy of sac-
rificing our *physical* existence to any thing inferior,
and to look upon it as that to which all other ends
are to be made subservient; but we grow up and
grow old without ever discerning a far more cunning
fallacy for which the other was but a preparatory
step, and we live on, merging the *thought* of our
being in its daily accidents, and immolating the life

of the spirit before the idol of its desires. Instead
of this, we should be quickening by our daily life
that spiritual consciousness which otherwise, in the
hour of death, we shall feel that we have lost; when
the eye that saw, and the ear that heard, have done
their tasks ; when the heavens which that eye has so
long gazed upon are rolling together as a scroll, and
the thousand tones of music which the ear has drank
from the earth are hushed, and the affrighted soul
turns inward upon itself as the sole remaining mon-
ument of all that was once real. Was such a con-
sciousness ours, then indeed might we sympathize
with Shakspeare ; then might the lofty thought which
Milton felt in his blindness and age, forever permeate
our being, and lift us to that height from which, like
him, we could look down on the world and the ob-
jects of sense beneath ; and as we gazed with the
soul's pure eyes, and a mind irradiated with that
celestial light for which he prayed, we too might
exclaim

> " For who would lose,
> Though full of pain, this intellectual being,
> These thoughts that wander through eternity,
> To perish rather swallowed up and lost
> In the wide womb of uncreated night,
> Devoid of sense and motion?"

This activity of mind in Shakspeare, to which the

4

theatre perhaps in some measure gave a direction, and the strong sense of life which must necessarily have accompanied it, leads us to the negation of the two, as the idea on which his mind would dwell most frequently and with the most concern. We find this thought therefore standing out more or less prominently throughout all his plays, and forming, as I have before said, the ground-plan of Hamlet. I cannot help quoting in this connection a passage from "As You Like It," which only Shakspeare could have written. The words are so simple that a fool might have uttered them, though only the wisest of men knew it. Yet none could impress upon us more strongly the fact that we live, and that

> "All that live must die
> Passing through nature to eternity."

> "A fool, a fool!—I met a fool i' the forest,
> A motley fool;—a miserable world!—
> As I do live by food, I met a fool;
> Who laid him down and bask'd him in the sun,
> And railed on lady Fortune in good terms,
> In good set terms,—and yet a motley fool.
> Good-morrow, fool, quoth I: No, sir, quoth he,
> Call me not fool, till heaven hath sent me fortune:
> And then he drew a dial from his poke;
> And looking on it with lack-lustre eye
> Says, very wisely, It is ten o'clock:

Thus may we see, quoth he, how the world wags:
'Tis but an hour ago, since it was nine ;
And after an hour more, 'twill be eleven ;
And so from hour to hour, we ripe and ripe,
And then, from hour to hour, we rot, and rot,
And thereby hangs a tale."

These feelings caused Shakspeare to live beyond the
influence of fame, and, though disturbed, as we have
shown, by the thought of *where* or *how* he might
exist in another world, he still felt the fact; and
fame can only be a motive to those who have no
practical belief in the next world, or to whom it is
an uncertainty. With the celebrated minds of anti-
quity, this was the case ; and they found in the
thought of fame some consolation for that activity
and sense of life which they felt to be their great
attributes, as if, that living tongues should tell of their
existence, was nearest to life itself. Think not that
it is for the paltry praise of others, that such have
lived and suffered ; believe it not, even though they
themselves knew not the spirit they were of, and in
their ignorance believed it ; no — it could not be ; —
it was the promptings of an *immortal* nature that
urged them to live, — to live, though it were to be but
a thought in the memory of others. In this yearning
of the spirit for being, for immortality, is seen a sign
of its relationship to God ; that it is in very deed the

child of the great I AM, and that in these its aspirations it calls Him Father. And as age on age rolls by, and we learn more humbly to bow to him who came to bring life and immortality to light, we shall feel more the truth of that sublime revelation which God early made of himself to his children, when he said to Moses, I Am that I Am.

From what has been said we may perceive that universality is not the gift of Shakspeare alone, but natural to the mind of man; and that whenever we unburthen ourselves of that load of selfishness under which what is natural in us lies distorted, it will resume as its own estate that diversity of being in which he delighted. That which in the poet, the philosopher, or the warrior, therefore affects us, is this higher natural action of the mind, which, though exhibited in one, is felt to be harmonious with all; which imparts to us, as it were, their own universality, and makes us for a while companions of their various life. In the individual act we feel more than that which suffices for this alone; we feel sensible that the blood that is filling one vein, and becoming visible to us in one form, possesses a vitality of which every limb and the whole body are alone the fit expression. This natural action of the mind is ever revealing to us more than we have before known in whatever direction applied, for this alone unconsciously moves in its appointed path; the only human actor in the drama of existence, save him who is by duty becoming consciously natural, that can show us any good. In its equable and uninterrupted movements, it harmonizes ever with nature, giving the spiritual interpretation to her silent and sublime growth. In the movements of Shakspeare's mind, we are permitted to see an explanation of that strange phenomenon in the government of Him who made us, by which that which is most universal appears to be coincident with that which is most particular. In him we see how it is that the mighty laws which bind system upon system should be the same that stoop to order with exactest precision the particles whose minuteness escapes our vision; that could we but feel aright, we should see that the same principle which teaches us to love ourselves, could not but lead us to love our neighbors as ourselves; that did we love in ourselves what was truly worthy of our love, there would be no object throughout the wide circle of being, whose lot and happiness would not be our own. It is thus by becoming most universal, we at the same time become most individual; for they are not opposed to each other, but different faces of the same thing. But selfishness is the farthest removed of all things from the universality of genius or of goodness. For as the superiority to the objects of sense which the soul naturally has, and which, when lost, love would restore, diminishes;

these senseless objects in their turn become masters; we are the servants of sin, bowing to an idol that our own hands have set up, and sweating beneath the burthens of a despot strong in our own transferred power. Like the ancients we too find a deity in each of the objects we pursue ; — we follow wealth till we worship Mammon ; love, till we see a Venus ; are ambitious, till our hands are stained with the bloody rites of Mars. While in the physical world we are waging by our rail-roads and engines a war of utter extermination against time and space, we forget that it is these very things, as motives, that urge us on. We are exhibiting the folly of kingdoms divided against themselves ; for, while in the physical world we are driving to annihilation space and time, it is for the very sake of the things of time and sense that we do it. We are thereby excluding ourselves daily from those *many* mansions which Christ has taught are prepared for us. Our words confess that all things are God's, while our hands are busy in fencing off some corner of the wide universe from which to exclude our brother man.

In the exceptions of our race, in those we have been accustomed to call great, we see universality claimed for them in their minds' own inborn and free-working energies. But others are more free agents, that they may not act unconsciously ; and that a conscious natural action when attained may be the eternal reward of their well doing. The mind which of its own inborn force is natural, is innocent; but that which has been permitted to become so, is virtuous. True virtue would be conscious genius. To minds in both of these states does universality belong; in the one, it is that of the child; in the other, that of manhood. Both are in harmony with nature. In the language of our Lord, they are little children learning to repeat the words they hear the Father utter. It was the same Father that fashioned him who wears a crown, and the shaggy monarch of the forest, who could alone give the corresponding state in the mind of a Shakspeare; which enabled him to be with the ease and naturalness of a Proteus, now " every inch a king," and now to be the lion too, and " roar so as to do any man's heart good to hear him; so that the Duke would say ' let him roar again, let him roar again.'" As the spontaneous action of Shakspeare's mind was continually finding an answering expression in the world around it, so must the same action in us, when restored by love, find the same ever-varied forms. We shall become all things to all men. As the wind bloweth where it listeth, and we hear the sound thereof, but cannot tell whence it cometh and whither it goeth, so passive will the breath of life that God first breathed into us become to his holy will. Life will be a continued worship, for every object will be a gift, and every gift an opportunity for love. When all men shall so live and speak, their souls will have consciously become the passive instruments of the Divine will; and will ever tell, in pure and spiritual worship to each other, the works and ways of a common Father. The highest exercise of the human will, will be formed in its assent to the Divine, Genius will be the obedience of the child; virtue, the obedience of the man to the same Universal Parent. The unconscious utterings of our poet will be found verified in himself.

" He that of greatest works is finisher,
　　Oft does them by the weakest minister:
　　So holy writ in babes hath judgment shown,
　　When judges have been babes. Great floods have
　　　　flown
　　From simple sources; and great seas have dried
　　When miracles have by the greatest been denied.
　　But most it is presumption in us, when
　　The help of heaven we count the acts of men."

So difficult is it therefore for us to forget ourselves, and to take our neighbor's situation with the same readiness that we hold our own, that we wonder very much at what we call Shakspeare's universality, his power of adapting himself to his characters; and that we see nothing of himself in them. The diffi-

culty that we imagine, and the want of perception
of the poet in his characters, are both a difficulty
and a want of our own making. Living, as we do, as
if we were made for the objects around us, and not
they for us, we are incapacitated for understanding
or seeing as an individual, one to whom no such in-
dividuality as we are conversant with belongs. We
are looking for one like ourselves, to whom we may
give a local habitation and a name; whom we may
call a lover of wealth, or pleasure, or fame, and forget
that to him whom we seek, places and names were
but toys. We see not nor understand that each of
the characters we read is the poet's, and that while
there, he neither wishes to be, nor is elsewhere. We
cannot better picture to our minds the dramatic state
of Shakspeare's, than by recalling to our thoughts
the days of our childhood, before we had been
schooled by the selfishness of sin, when the tides of
life flowed on with no will but His who was pouring
them through our souls. Then was it, as has been
said, that man "filled nature with his overflowing
currents." Could we deny the false pride which
springs from the exercise of our own wills, could
we submit them in humbleness to Him in whom we
should live and move and have *our* being, we should
still feel in manhood and age that our's was that
universal life and love, the emblem of which our
Saviour beheld in a little child, and said "of such is

the kingdom of heaven." This period in youth we call natural; all that the child does bears the impress of universal life; like Adam, he is unconsciously the lord of creation; he is content with living; his happiness has not yet become the selfish love of possession; his actions and thoughts are full of life unclaimed save by Him who gave it. Like the Greek, the past and future tenses are with him present; he is what he describes, and his gestures mark actions as if he saw them and was pointing them out in the vacuity. To Shakspeare's whole life we might apply the same language that we do in speaking of the frolics of a child, — how full he is of life! — this is that which is most apparent in his every character. The stronger this activity, the more happiness is there in the mind's own exercise, the more is it independent of the particular object on which its power is exerted, and the more coincident is it with all forms of being. In every actor in the mighty drama of human existence, did Shakspeare find himself; he wished to live and move, and this was Shakspeare. He was rich, he was poor, he was wise, he was foolish, he was mad, he was sober, "desiring this man's art and that man's scope," each and all, yet neither. He lived as each character, yet was not that which at any one time appeared, since that which is individual can only be a face of the universal. In each, he might say, with Iago, " I

am not that I am." I cannot farther illustrate this
childlike action of his mind better than by applying
to him what Wordsworth has said of a child.

" Behold the child among his new-born blisses,
    A six years' Darling of a pigmy size!
    See, where 'mid work of his own hand he lies,
    Fretted by sallies of his mother's kisses,
    With light upon him from his father's eyes,
    See at his feet some little plan or chart,
    Some fragment from his dream of human life
    Shaped by himself with newly-learned art;
        A wedding or a festival,
        A mourning or a funeral;
            And this hath now his heart,
        And unto this he frames his song;
            Then will he fit his tongue
    To dialogues of business, love, or strife,
            But it will not be long
            Ere this be thrown aside,
            And with new joy and pride
    The little actor cons another part,
    Filling from time to time his " humorous stage"
    With all the Persons down to palsied age,
    That Life brings with her in her equipage;
        As if his whole vocation
        Were endless imitation."

In this activity of mind, then, in this childlike
superiority to the objects by which it was attracted,
we find Shakspeare. This was his genius, for genius
is nothing but this natural action of the mind ren-
dering obedient to itself by a higher principle those
objects to whose power it might otherwise have been
subjected. This it was that enabled him like a boy
" to toss creation like a bauble from hand to hand,
embodying in turn each capricious shade of thought."
Thus it was, that, while others were making ends of
things, he gave to them their deeper significance of
life and death, of time, and eternity. In this view,
the acts of Shakspeare seem but natural movements.
With the ever-surprised mind of a child, he was
always transformed into the object he saw. This
condition of mind might perhaps be designated as
an impersonal one, so strongly is it always possessed
by that which is before it, as to seem for the time to
have no other individuality. It is the unconscious
possessor of all things, and, like the mythological
Greek, gives personality and voice even to the objects
of inanimate creation. This is that primæval state
of innocence from which we have fallen. We are
no longer carried out of ourselves to become the
expression of that which is around us; but enchained
by our own wills, the cloud and the flower speak
only through our dictation. Would we attain to the
recognition of the individuality of a Shakspeare or

a Homer, (for they had an individuality and one
which it shames us not to perceive,) it can only be
by being born again, by becoming again through
obedience as little children, and by feeling more
fully than we have yet done the meaning of that
sublime declaration of our Lord's, "all that the
Father hath is mine."

As we arrive in our own consciousness at a truer
perception of what Shakspeare was, we shall start
with strange wonder to see how far we have strayed
from the paths of our youth, how much we have
substituted calculation for right, selfishness for love.
We shall then be surprised that we ever sought for
him apart from his creations, and learn that the per-
fect poet is never visible save in action, in the ever new,
ever changing aspect of nature and of man. Truth
and time are separate rays only when seen through
the medium of an imperfect act; but through the
perfect and entire action of the mind they are seen
blended in the life as primary colors in the common
light of day.

This view of Shakspeare will lead us to look upon
his characters as the natural expression of his own,
as its necessary growths or offshoots. We shall then
see a reason for their being as they actually appear
to be facts, real events; which you could no more
alter or improve, than you can the branch of a tree,
or the visible realities themselves. Such being the

foundations on which his characters rest, we may see
why it is that they stand in the front of mental
achievements ; and that we speak and think of them
as those with whom we are acquainted, whom we
have seen and addressed. " We talk," says Charles
Lamb, " of Shakspeare's admirable observation of
life, when we should feel that not from a petty inqui-
sition into those cheap and every-day characters
which surrounded him as they surround us ; but
from his own mind, which was, to borrow a phrase
of Ben Jonson's, the very " sphere of humanity,"
he fetched those images of virtue and of knowledge,
of which every one of us recognising a part, think
we comprehend in our natures the whole, and often-
times mistake the powers which he positively creates
in us for nothing more than indigenous faculties of
our own minds, which only wanted the application
of corresponding virtues in him to return a full and
clear echo of the same." We may study a char-
acter, notice its incomings and its outgoings, and,
having become perfectly acquainted with the whole
whereabout of its life, may place it in a given situation,
and put the words that it would be sure to utter in
its mouth ; and, after all, it would be no more like the
breathing life of one of Shakspeare's characters than
the merest wire-strung automaton. Such a form has
no counterpart in creation ; it is as dead as the soul
that made it. We have, it may be, copied with

weary finger and wisest head the mere letter of life, but our hearts have been far from the task; and the mental abortion will go but to increase the number of those " gorgons, hydras and chimeras dire" with which the fruitful loins of the press over-teem. Each of the characters that Shakspeare has left us, on the contrary, was his own; the impulse by which he moved was so universal that it rendered his being coincident with that of all. He actually lived what he represented. We cannot speak of him as breaking away from his own egotism and throwing himself into his characters; he had no egotism other than that which would arise from that childlike state of mind, which robes itself in no particular shape, but in all shapes. For him everything lives and moves. For him, as for those of our race who spoke the early Shemitic language, there were no neuter nouns.

" I am the sea; hark, how her sighs do blow!
She is the weeping welkin, I the earth :
Then must my sea be moved with her sighs;
Then must my earth with her continual tears
Become a deluge, overflowed and drowned."

It may seem strange that a mind capable of the conception, as we call it, of a Hamlet or a Lear should yet seem to delight in those apparently so

opposite, — in characters of a low or even licentious
cast. But this apparent inconsistency admits of an
easy explanation from the very nature of that mind's
action. To us indeed they seem antipodes ; but to
him they stood embraced by the same horizon of
life and action. If we will but think of his mind as
moved by the same desire of action as our own
limbs are in childhood, and with as little end in view
save that of its own activity ; we shall then easily
conceive why he should seek to identify himself
with every mode of life, and be and act characters
of the most apparently opposite nature. That such
was the impulse under which they were written, we
can only appeal to each one's consciousness in read-
ing for a proof. He delighted in all men of high
as well as low estate, — we had almost said, in the
licentious as in the virtuous. But how different is
that playful and childlike spirit with which he acted
a vicious character, from that which seems to have
actuated a Byron. The one represents an aban-
doned man as he actually exists, with the joys of
sense and the anguish of the spirit alternately agitat-
ing his troubled breast; and the contemplation of
such a character, if it does not make us as good as
it might have done, had he drawn it with higher
motives, will yet make us better, as the sight of it
does in actual life. But the latter was not innocent,
he imparted something of himself to what he de-

scribes; he would not and could not, like Shakspeare, put before us a virtuous man with the same pleasure as he does a vicious one ; he has not, like him, held a pure and untarnished mirror up to nature, but reflected her back upon us from his own discolored and passion stained bosom.

Shakspeare acted like his own Falstaff " on instinct"; no ligament save that of existence bound him to any particular mode of action. We cannot therefore learn the moral influence which his writings have had upon society, and the effect of this or that character or passage from what seem to us their consequences, unless, at the same time, we are conscious of the state of mind from which they proceeded. There may have been a deeper instinct or principle at work in the poet's mind by which those very consequences we blame were fashioned to be the instruments of good. Of this we can learn only by our lives. The rugged summits of virtue alone command the prospect over the plains of innocence ; and true manhood can alone interpret the sports of the child. It is from this central position only that we may hope to trace aright the orbit of his influence and the moral tendency of his writings. He lived in thought as we live in sense ; what the involuntary movements of our bodies are to us, the action of his mind was to him ; and as it darted " from heaven to earth, from earth to heaven," the wide

5

world seemed but the green play-ground of his
youth, and our long years of life a summer's day.
This difference is well shown by the choruses of
acts third and fifth in King Henry V.

> " *Thus, with imagined wing, our swift scene flies,*
>   *In motion of no less celerity*
>   *Than that of thought.* Suppose that you have seen
>   The well-appointed king at Hampton pier
>   Embark his royalty ; and his brave fleet
>   With silken streamers the young Phœbus fanning,
>   *Play with your fancies ; and in them behold,*
>   Upon the hempen tackle, ship-boys climbing :
>   Hear the shrill whistle, which doth order give
>   To sounds confused : behold the threaden sails,
>   Borne with the invisible and creeping wind,
>   Draw the huge bottoms through the furrowed sea,
>   Breasting the lofty surge :   *O, do but think,*
>   You stand upon the rivage, and behold
>   A city on the inconstant billows dancing ;
>   *For so appears this fleet majestical,*
>   *Holding due course to Harfleur.   Follow, follow!*
>   *Grapple your minds to sternage of this navy ;*
>   And leave your England as dead midnight still,
>   Guarded with grandsires, babies and old women,
>   Either past, or not arrived to, pith and puissance :
>   For who is he, whose chin is but enriched
>   With one appearing hair, that will not follow

These culled and choice-drawn cavaliers **to**
    France?
Work, work, your thoughts, and therein see a siege!
Behold the ordnance on their carriages,
With fatal mouths gaping on girded Harfleur.
Suppose the ambassador from the French **comes**
    back;
Tells Harry — that the king doth offer him
Katharine his daughter; and with her, to dowry,
Some petty and unprofitable dukedom;
The offer likes not: and the nimble gunner,
With linstock now the devilish cannon touches,
And down goes all before him. Still be kind,
And eke out our performance with your mind."
                        Act 3d.

His mental life was as much a matter of impulse **as**
the restless activity of our youth. Other poets **we**
blame or praise, but Shakspeare only elicits **our**
wonder. He spent his life in living in thought the
lives of others. What he was and felt he said, **and**
it was nature and truth; for acting from impulse he
did not strive to build up character, according to **his**
own presumption, and preconceived notions, but **only**
described, as I have said, what he himself was **and**
felt in their positions as he severally occupied them.
He did not, like Corneille, hold back vice that **she**
might not speak her part, nor did he, like Byron, re-
strain virtue. No actor in life is driven from **his**

stage, and the consequence is, that, although he acted neither from a good or bad motive but only from instinct, he has produced for us, "in his quick forge and working-house of thought," a natural mental growth of those very events by which God in their ordinary course is teaching us; and which, by the action of his mind, he has again presented us for warning and pleasure abridged of their "huge and proper life."

The true influence of his characters as individuals and even as groups, then, is, that by them we are continually reminded of his own, of what we may call the impersonal state of childhood, a state which we have all known, yet from which we have all fallen; that condition of innocence in which lived our first parents, when all things were gifts, and they were one with them; for they were each the offering of Infinite Love. We do not look upon Shakspeare as purposing this or any other effect; but consider it as the unconscious influence of one ever active in the mental life of which we have spoken, and of which the words he has left us were but the natural acompaniment. We can impart but what we are, and Shakspeare formed no exception to that which binds all other men. As we converse with him, at every turn, in each of the varied forms under which he presents himself, we are ever wondering at and groping after that strange individuality from which they all proceed. This attained, we shall read the riddle of his character, and stand surprised within ourselves at the simplicity of the solution.

We look in vain therefore in Shakspeare for that consciousness of the unconquerable will that we find in Milton. Shakspeare could never have given us a character like Satan's. He has indeed made us feel in the impulses of our nature a depth and strength of which before we had scarcely any conception. The whispers of conscience and the prompting of natural affection seem at times to speak with almost supernatural power; and call upon the selfish and sin-stricken soul in tones that bear us back, as it were, to that mysterious moment, when the springs of our being were unsealed, and we hear again the streams of its murmuring life gushing from out their fountains. Thus when the thought that *so* her father looked, flashes across the murderous mind of Lady Macbeth, as she sees the gray locks and venerable face of the sleeping Duncan; it seems as if we saw the dark pall of clouds that have gathered with more than midnight blackness, over her devoted head, rent for an instant asunder, disclosing to her guilty soul, but one moment and the last, the blue bright heaven of her childhood's thoughts. But the wickedness of such an one as Lady Macbeth, and even Iago, we can pity and pardon; for we feel that under happier influences their nature would have been changed; it is the first sin of Adam, and not the full-grown conscious guilt of his tempter. Shakspeare represents man as he is; too weak to contend by his own unaided strength against the destroyer of our own race, unable of himself to find the way, the truth, and the light, yet needing their continual guidance. In Macbeth, the struggle for victory is still kept up, the fight is far from being ended, and the night is still on the approach;—but with Iago, it is past; the shadows have long since fallen over the field of his defeat; as we try to retrace its past history, all is indefinite, and the imagination fills its unknown extent with sights more terrific than any actual conflict could have presented; every object swells into unreal proportions, and at every step the night thickens with horrors around us. In his character we seem to see the conquest of sin complete, and the bondage of the spirit consummated; a state the more dreadful to our view since the dark field of conflict is hidden by the past; and we see the slave of sin sunk even below the remembrance of his freedom, and rejoicing in iniquity as if it was his natural heritage. But with Satan there is no joy in iniquity, he ever feels

> " How awful goodness is, and sees
> Virtue in her shape how lovely; sees and pines
> His loss."

Ever in his bosom gnaws the worm that dieth not; ever burns the fire that is not quenched. His is that sin unto death, for which we may not pray. It had been in vain had the very light of heaven shone around the darkness of the archangel; and we look with hate upon his gigantic iniquity, as upon a dæmon more than human; for whom there remains no place for repentance, and for whom is reserved the blackness of darkness forever.

·Since Shakspeare accomplished so great results without any apparent object, and since the strains of the bard are ever so welcome to the general ear; it has been inferred that his motive was to please. But that poetry gives pleasure, is a consequence of its being written, not the motive for it. We degrade those whom the world has pronounced poets, when we assume any other cause of their song than the divine and original action of the soul in humble obedience to the Holy Spirit upon whom they call. Wherever this action is, it is its own cause for being heard; for it is the word of God uttered through the soul as it ever speaks through inanimate creation. Homer and Shakspeare were without a struggle the natural representatives of this action; and they were a universal expression through which all things might utter themselves. They were the innocent and unconscious children of duty, and in the ode of Wordsworth, we read of them;

    " There are who ask not if thine eye
      Be on them; who, in love and truth
      Where no misgiving is, rely
      Upon the genial sense of youth :
      Glad Hearts ! without reproach or blot ;
      Who do thy work, and know it not :
      Long may the kindly impulse last !
  But thou, if they should totter, teach them to stand
         fast !"

Such minds, as we have before said, seem to be ex-
ceptions, for wise purposes, to the rest of our race;
exhibiting to all the natural features of the soul in
the unconscious and childlike state of innocence.
The world is theirs, but it is so only because they
are innocent ; and they describe it as if it had never
known sin. In Wordsworth and Milton, on the con-
trary, we see the struggle of the child to become the
perfect man in Christ Jesus. Their constant prayer
is, " not my will, Father, but thine be done." They
are striving for that silence in their own bosoms that
shall make the voice that created all things heard.
It is the self which opposes this, that they feel with-
in them and see without them ; and it is this alone,
under whatsoever forms it may be, that they describe.
They use not others' lips and words, because they
are their own, but only in the place of their own ; and
the language which their characters utter is not the

varying•personality of a Shakspeare, but the trans-
fered one of a single-sided individuality. Like the
fallen angel they cannot escape the consciousness of
themselves, and the brightness of poesy, instead of
blazing directly down upon their heads, causes them
from the obliqueness of its rays to be ever accompa-
nied by their own shadow. But when the war of
self which these and other bards have so nobly main-
tained shall have ceased, and the will of the Father
shall be done on earth as it is in heaven; when man
shall have come to love his neighbor as himself;
then shall the poet again find himself speaking with
many tongues; and the expectant nations shall listen
surprised to a note more sublime, yet accordant with
the rolling numbers of the Chian minstrel, and more
sweet than the wild warblings of the bard of Avon.
To the soul with whom striving has ceased, shall re-
turn that peace which makes all that God hath to be
ours. It shall speak in all the utterances of joy and
grief; and their full and perfect voice, which in-
nocence has failed to express, shall rise from the
deep bosom of its spiritual love. Virtue shall find
in genius her erring, though innocent child; and
genius shall follow in love her maternal guidance.
The few that have appeared first shall then seem
last; and the last shall be seen to be first. Each
soul shall show in its varied action the beauty and

grandeur of nature; and shall live forever a teacher of the words it hears from the Father.

Shakspeare's life, as we have endeavored to show, was coincident with that of others, from the natural action of his mind; and from its unreserved yielding to events it has exhibited them to us more as they are than any other mind has yet done. But a more perfect coincidence, which shall exhibit more of what man is than he has done, can only be brought about by feeling more deeply that all things are ours, and by possessing more of that love which knew what was in man. Had this, and a sense of duty been Shakspeare's, they would have rendered more powerful and affecting the influence of his characters without making them in any degree less natural. But it may be asked, should the poet be more moral than Providence; if he exhibit things as they are, will they not have all the influence that God intended they should have? It is that the poet should represent things as they are, for which we contend. We are not pleading for those sickly beings who, by the handy work of the mind, are made to fit any prescribed pattern of goodness; but for those who live and move about us; to describe the height and depth of whose thoughts and passions, and interpret their meaning, hidden it may be from themselves, even such a mind as Shakspeare's must have entered into and portrayed characters not only from impulse, but

also with a love whose strength was that of duty.
Too easily might we else, as he has sometimes done,
quicken with our life the dry bones of moral death
around us. It is no common lamp that will enable
us to thread securely the dark and labyrinthine cav-
erns of sin, to shed that light even amid its damp
and fatal vapors that will enable us to draw from
their lowest depths the rich treasures of wisdom
which they hide. No one can enter more entirely
into the lives of others than Shakspeare has done,
until he has laid down his own life, and gone forth
to seek and to save that which is lost. Our more
perfect views were not intended to be the substitutes
for, but the interpreters of the characters of others.
What ought to be, if we describe it by itself, be-
comes but our own teaching; what is, if we look
upon it with a spirit more nearly allied to His who
sees all things as they are, will prove the lessons not
of our own insignificance, but of His providence.
We need not substitute our ideals of virtue and vice
for the living forms around us; we need not brighten
the one, nor darken the other; to the spiritual eye,
even here, will the just begin to appear as angels of
light; and as the sun of Divine Favor sets on the
wicked, their lengthening shadows, even here, are
seen to blacken and dilate into more gigantic and aw-
ful proportions. Shakspeare's characters are true
and natural indeed; but they are not the truest and

most natural which the world will yet see. From
the states of mind of a Hamlet and Macbeth, rise
tones of which the words he has made them utter,
bear but faint intelligence; and which will find a
stronger and yet stronger utterance as the will of the
poet conforms to that of his Maker. Shakspeare
was gifted with the power of the poet; a power
which, though he may have employed for the pur-
poses intended, does not seem to have been ac-
companied by that sense of responsibility which
would have lent them their full and perfect effect. His
creations are natural, but they are unconsciously so.
He could but give to them his own life, which was
one of impulse and not of principle. Man's brightest
dignity is conscious nature; and virtue when depriv-
ed of this is robbed of her nobility; and without it vice
is but a pardonable weakness. Shakspeare is not to
be esteemed so much a man, as a natural phenom-
enon. We cannot say of him that he conformed to
God's will; but that the Divine Will in its ordinary op-
erations moved his mind as it does the material world.
He was natural from an unconscious obedience to the
will of God; *we*, if it acts not so strongly upon us
but has left us the greater freedom, must become
natural by a conscious obedience to it. He that is
least in the kingdom of heaven, is greater than he.

To show with what different effect his mind would
have acted had it been deeply affected by the truths

of Christianity ; and the consequent imperfections which his creations must exhibit to a mind so affected, is evidently to be done not so much by precept, as by example, not so much by criticism on his, as by other characters of one's own. That to a mind of his power, virtue and vice would have had a deeper, and in no wise less natural signification from the superadded light of Revelation, no one, we think, can doubt. Our own souls must be rendered a fit medium of those spiritual conflicts we are listening to in the breasts of others ; else, some of the sounds which would otherwise come clear and distinct will fall faint and unmeaning, and others will be entirely lost to our spiritual ear. Shakspeare's mind was, as we have said, a pure and spotless mirror in which to reflect nature ; but it was the purity and spotlessness of innocence, and not of virtue. Had that love of action which was so peculiarly the motive of Shakspeare's mind been followed also as a duty, it would have added a strength to his characters which we do not feel them now to possess. They are, it is true, natural, but they are no more than nature. However amiable our feelings, — the common bonds of humanity, — they are weak as flaxen cords in the giant hands of our selfishness, unless strengthened by duty. Even a mother, whose heart is knit to her offspring in what would seem the closest of all natural ties, can,

when her own selfish ends have made conquest of
her soul, exclaim,

> " I have given suck; and know
> How tender 'tis, to love the babe that milks me:
> I would, while it was smiling in my face,
> Have plucked my nipple from his boneless gums,
> And dashed the brains out, had I so sworn as you
> Have done to this,"

Such and so weak is poor human nature. Had it not
been so, a revelation of higher motives would not
have been needed or given. Had Shakspeare felt
these, his characters would have been more con-
sciously natural. For the erring, he would have made
us feel a deeper pity ; for the wicked, a stronger aver-
sion ; and for the virtuous, a more enduring love. He
would have made us feel that sinning as we do in
the light both of nature and revelation, we should
still continue to sin even amid the full broad blaze of
heaven.

In Shakspeare's works, I see but the ordinary pow-
er of the Deity acting in mind, as I see it around me
moulding to its purpose the forms of matter. But
we are too apt to admire as the *man* that which we
should only regard as the natural operation of the
Divine Power. Struck with wonder by this natural
action of the mind, we are too prone to dignify as

that image of the Most High in which we were crea-
ted, something which no more deserves the appella-
tion of man, than the clod on which we tread.   To
be natural either consciously or unconsciously, is in-
deed alone to be truly great; for that which is so is
God's.   The material world, and to a hardly less
extent the mental one of those we call great, are
passive beneath his influence; they are naturally,
but unconsciously so.   But man is gifted with a will
whose highest exercise could he but recognise the
awfulness of the trust, he would feel to be its per-
fect accordance with his Maker's.   But even from
the first moment of his existence, when he dared
disobedience to his conscience, he became unnatural;
and the fair Eden in which he was placed seemed
no longer his home; and he is driven a wanderer
through his own Fatherland, and lets himself out as
a hired servant to till those very fields which were
once his own.   To become natural, to find again that
Paradise which he has lost, man must be born again,
he must learn that the true exercise of his own will
is only in listening to that voice which is ever walking
in the garden, but of which he is afraid and hides
himself.   In the words of him who came not to do
his own will, as we humble ourselves and become as
little children, our minds will no longer be at vari-
ance with the world without them; but only a bright-
er image than nature can be of the creator of both;

the true soul will be the conscious expression of na-
ture. Shakspeare was natural; but, if we may judge
from his writings and life, he must have been as un-
consciously so as a field or a stream. As we have
said, he was not moved by common motives; he
wished but to live, and he passed without a prefer-
ence through all the forms of living, and may be
said to have been most truly himself in being others.
Had he pursued the same course from a sense of
duty, there would have been added to his characters
that strength of will, or remorse at its loss in which
we feel them especially wanting. That he acted
from impulse and not from principle, shows us that
he is not to be regarded as a man so much as a phe-
nomenon; that the tribute he would ask was admiration
rather than praise. The careless manner in which he
left his works has been wondered at, and lauded
long enough, we hope, for christian men. When will
we learn that the thing we call a man wants that
which alone can entitle it to that appellation, when he
can think a thought, or do a single act, much less
leave the works of a whole life with ostrich-like in-
difference on the barren sands of a world's neglect,
without one look behind at their influence on the eter-
nal happiness or misery of all being. 'Twas God's
care only that the mind he sent labored not in vain.
Action, in which God's will is not the motive, is
sending the lightning flashes of heaven to play for

men's amusement among the far-off clouds; and not to flash in warning across the dark path of destruction in which they are treading. It is the successive peals of thunder which, instead of purifying the moral atmosphere, are made to roll and burst only to create vainly repeated echoes among the hills. Shakspeare, though at times he may have been possessed of this genius, must, in far the most numerous of his days and years, have been possessed by it. Lost in wonder at the countless beings that thronged uncalled the palace of his soul, and dwelt beneath its "majestical roof fretted with golden fires;" he knew not, or if he knew, forgot that even those angel visitants were not sent for him merely to admire and number; but that knowing no will but His who made kings his subjects, he should send them forth on their high mission, and with those high resolves which it was left for him to communicate. Had he done this, we might indeed reverence him as the image of his God; as a sharer in His service, whose service is perfect freedom.

From God's action in the mind of such men, we may learn, though with less clearness, that great lesson of Humility which He has revealed through his word. From genius, as well as revelation, we learn that our actions can alone become harmonious with the universality and naturalness which we see in the outward world, when they are made to accord

6

with the will of our Father. From both we learn, that of ourselves we can do no positive act; but have only the power given us to render of no avail that which is so — that we cannot make one hair white or black; that our seeming strength is weakness, nay, worse than weakness, unless it co-operates with God's. Let us labor then, knowing that the more we can erase from the tablets of our hearts the false fashions and devices which our own perverse wills have written over them, the more will shine forth, with all their original brightness, those ancient primeval characters, traced there by the finger of God, until our whole being is full of light.

HAMLET.

THE play of Hamlet, when viewed with reference
to the character of Shakspeare, which we have
given, will no longer stand in that unique relation to
the rest of his performances it has hitherto held ; but
will be found to be more vitally connected, than any
of them, with the great characteristics of the poet's
mind. We have chosen this, therefore, because it
illustrates our previous remarks ; and because these,
in their turn, afford the position from which it is to
be viewed. As to the time of its composition, it
stands at about an equal distance between his first
and last play ; and, we think, we can see the influ-
ence of this upon those that succeed, in giving them
more of a sobered and tragical interest. Those
who have attempted an explanation of it, have failed
from the want of a just conception of Hamlet's
situation and character. In Lear, and in many other

of Shakspeare's plays, the chief character seems
naturally to be that for which all the others were
formed ; and, however important these are at first,
as objects for the eye to rest on, they seem, at last,
to the mind, but as shadings to show the main one in
the strongest light.   This is especially the case with
Hamlet ; and they who have commented on it, seem
to have erred from viewing that as of the greatest
importance, which Shakspeare must have considered
but as accidental.   There is, to use his own words,
" *something more than natural*" in this tragedy, " if
philosophy could find it out."   That which makes it
so, is the playing up, in a peculiar manner, of the
great features of Shakspeare's own mind — that sense
of existence which must have been, as we have said,
the accompanying state of so much and so varied ac-
tivity.   Hence the darkness which has so long hung
over it ; a darkness which, for us, can only be dis-
pelled, when we too rest on the same simple basis.

Instead of feeling, continually, that the life is
more than the food, and the body than the raiment;
we live as if it were directly the other way, and by
that very state of mind, are incapacitated almost
from conceiving of one who stood in a truer relation
to things ; to whose thoughts, time and space seem
not to adhere as to ours — who could " put a girdle
round about the earth in forty minutes," and to whom
this, our life of years, was but " a bank and shoal of

time." From the soul of him upon whom Christian-
ity has had its true effect, as from before the face of
him whom John saw in vision, sitting upon "a great
white throne," "the earth and the heavens have fled
away, and there is found no place for them." Shaks-
peare was, as I have said, the childlike embodyment
of this sense of existence. It found its *natural* ex-
pression in the many forms of his characters; in
the circumstances of Hamlet, its *peculiar* one. As
has been well observed, the others we love for some-
thing that may be called adventitious; but we love
him not, we think not of him because he was witty,
because he is melancholy, but because he existed
and was himself; this is the sum total of the impres-
sion. The great fore-plane of adversity has been
driven over him, and his soul is laid bare to the very
foundation. It is here that the poet is enabled to
build deep down on the clear ground-work of being.
It is because the interest lies here, that Shakspeare's
own individuality becomes more than usually promi-
nent. We here get down into his deep mind, and
the thoughts that interested him, interest us. Here
is where our Shakspeare suffered, and, at times, a
golden vein of his own fortune penetrates to the sur-
face of Hamlet's character, and enriches, with a new
value, the story of his sorrows.

If Shakspeare's master passion then was, as we
have seen it to be, the love of intellectual activity

for its own sake, his continual satisfaction with the
simple pleasure of existence must have made him
more than commonly liable to the fear of death ; or,
at least, made that change the great point of interest
in his hours of reflection. Often and often must he
have thought, that, to be or not to be forever, was a
question, which must be settled ; as it is the founda-
tion, and the only foundation upon which we feel that
there can rest one thought, one feeling, or one pur-
pose worthy of a human soul. Other motives had
no hold upon him ; — place, riches, favors, the prizes
of accident, he could lose and still exclaim, " For-
tune and I are friends," but the thought of death
touched him in his very centre. However strong
the sense of continued life such a mind as his may
have had, it could never reach that assurance of
eternal existence, which Christ alone can give, —
which alone robs the grave of victory, and takes
from death its sting. Here lie the materials out of
which this remarkable tragedy was built up. From
the wrestling of his own soul with the great enemy,
comes that depth and mystery which startles us in
Hamlet.

It is to this condition that Hamlet has been re-
duced. This is the low portal of grief to which we
must stoop, before we can enter the heaven-pointing
pile that the poet has raised to his memory. Stun-
ned by the sudden storm of woes, he doubts, as he

looks at the havoc spread around him, whether he
himself is left, and fears lest the very ground on
which he lies prostrate, may not prove treacherous.
Stripped of all else, he is sensible on this point alone.
Here is the life from which all else grows. Inter-
ested in the glare of prosperity around him, only be-
cause he lives, he is ever turning his eyes from it to
the desolation in which he himself stands. His
glance ever descends from the lofty pinnacle of pride
and false security to the rotten foundation, — and
tears follow smiles. He raises his eye to heaven,
and "this brave o'erhanging firmament" seems to him
but "a pestilential congregation of vapors;" it de-
scends to earth, and "its goodly frame seems a sterile
promontory." He fixes it on man, and his noble apos-
trophe — "what a piece of work is a man! How
noble in reason! How infinite in faculties, in form
and moving, how express and admirable! in action,
how like an angel! in apprehension, how like a
god!" is followed fast upon by the sad confession,
"Yet man delights me not, nor woman neither."
He does not, as we say, "get accustomed to his sit-
uation." He holds fast by the wisdom of afflic-
tion, and will not let her go. He would keep her,
for she is his life. The storm has descended, and
all has been swept away but the rock. To this he
clings for safety. He will not return, like the dog to
his vomit. He will not render unavailing the les-

sons of Providence by "getting accustomed" to feed
on that which is not bread, on which to live is death.
He fears nothing save the loss of existence.   But
this thought thunders at the very base of the cliff
on which, ship-wrecked of every other hope, he had
been thrown.   That which to every body else seems
common, presses upon him with an all-absorbing in-
terest; he struggles with the mystery of his own
being, the root of all other mysteries, until it has
become an overmastering element in his own mind,
before which all others yield and seem as nothing.

This is the hinge on which his every endeavor
turns.   Such a thought as this might well prove more
than an equal counterpoise to any incentive to what
we call action.   The obscurity that lies over these
depths of Hamlet's character, arises from this unique
position in which the poet exhibits him; a position
which opens to us the basis of Shakspeare's own be-
ing, and which, though dimly visible to all, is yet
familiar to but few.   There is action indeed, but pro-
jected on so gigantic a scale, that, like the motion of
some of the heavenly bodies, from whom we are in-
conceivably removed, it seems a perpetual rest.
With Dr. Johnson, and other commentators, we are
at first inclined to blame Hamlet's inactivity, and call
him weak and cowardly; but as we proceed, and
his character and situation open upon us, such epi-
thets seem least of all applicable to him.   So far is

he from being a coward, in the common meaning of
that term, that he does not set this life at a pin's
fee. He is contending in thought with the great
realities beyond it — the dark clouds that hang over
the valley of the shadow of death, and float but dim-
ly and indistinct before *our* vision, have, like his
father's ghost, become fixed and definite " in *his*
mind's eye ;" he has looked them into shape, and
they stand before him wherever he turns, with a pres-
ence that will not be put by. Thus it is, that to
most he seems a coward, and that enterprises which
to others appear of great pith and moment,

" With this regard, their currents turn awry
    And lose the name of action."

Macbeth is contending with the realities of this world,
Hamlet with those of the next. The struggle which
is going on in the far-seeing mind of Hamlet never
arrives at its consummation ; Macbeth, on the con-
trary, is short-sighted enough to contend with the
whips and scorns of time, and with him, therefore,
the mental conflict is soon over.

" If it were done, when 'tis done, then 'twere well
    It were done quickly : If the assassination
    Could trammel up the consequence, and catch
    With his surcease success ; that but this blow

> Might be the be-all and the end-all *here*,
> But here upon this bank and shoal of time
> We'd jump *the life to come*."

But it may be asked, if Hamlet valued this life so
cheaply, nay, even meditated self-slaughter, why,
when he had an opportunity of dying by only suffer-
ing himself to be carried to England, he should fly
that very death he before sought? To this question,
the state of his mind affords us a satisfactory answer ;
and his wavering does but confirm our belief in his
sincerity, and give us a still stronger proof, that al-
though there is nothing from which he would more
willingly part withal — except, as he says, " my
life," yet still does the deep instinct of his soul
prompt him to retain it, though crushed by the bur-
den, while he doubts lest with its loss, may not be
connected the loss of all being. He cared not, as
he says, for *this* little life, a pin's fee ; but for life it-
self, his whole nature called in cries that would not
be silenced. In his perplexity and doubt, Hamlet
had interrogated his own nature on the great ques-
tion of his future being ; but its only response was
— " the dread of something after death ;" that some-
thing might be annihilation, or,

> " To lie in cold obstruction, and to rot.
> ———— or to be worse than worst

Of those, that lawless and uncertain thoughts
Imagine howling."

In the bitterness of his spirit, but half concealed by
his jests in the graveyard, he asks again that ques-
tion from which he cannot escape, sending his voice
down into the hollow tomb, and hearing but the echo
of his own words in reply. He loved not this life,
yet endured and clung to it because he doubted of
another ; this it was

> " That made calamity of so long life,
> And made him rather bear those ills he had
> Than fly to others that he knew not of."

This doubt still remained after all his reasoning;
and, gathering strength at the moment of death's ac-
tual approach, led him, like the old man with the
bundle of sticks, to deny that he had summoned him.

This view will account for Hamlet's indecision.
With him the next world, by the intense action of
his thoughts, had become as real as the present;
and, whenever this is the case, thought must always
at first take precedence of action. We have said at
first, for it ends in giving the strength of the spirit to
the arm of flesh. Hamlet frequently accuses him-
self of cowardice and indecision, yet is fully con-
scious, at the same time, of faultlessness. We too

go with him, and at first accuse him of it, and after-
wards rest in as full a conviction as he himself, that
he is not a coward. Could we view him from the
position in which Shakspeare must have seen him,
he would appear a hero of loftier stature and nobler
action, than any other that now wins our admiration
from among his numberless creations. Had we
Shakspeare's eye, we should not so much be touched
by the mere outward show of madness and inaction,
but looking beyond these at the deeper meaning,
should exclaim,

> " O, what a noble mind is here!
>   The courtier's, soldier's, scholar's, eye, tongue,
>   sword,
>   The expectancy and rose of the fair state,
>   The glass of fashion, and the mould of form,
>   The observed of all observers!"

Then too might we understand the delicate and hid-
den satire in that comparison which he makes be-
tween himself and Fortinbras.

> " Witness this army of such mass and charge,
>   Led by a delicate and tender prince,
>   Whose spirit with divine ambition puff'd,
>   Makes mouths at the *in*visible event;
>   Exposing what is mortal and unsure,

To all that fortune, death and danger dare
Even for an egg-shell."

Even the revenge which suggests itself to Hamlet is
not of this world. To others it would assume a
character of the most savage enormity, and one
from which, of all men, the tender and conscientious
prince would soonest shrink. But with him it is as
natural as his most ordinary action. He has looked
through the slight afflictions of this world, and his
prophetic eye is fixed on the limitless extent beyond.
Here and here alone, will the fire of the king's in-
cestuous lust burn unquenched, and the worm of re-
morse never die. Hence are heard the words that
seem to rise from a fiendish depth in the bosom.

" Up sword and know thou a more horrid hent :
When he is drunk, asleep, or in his rage."

We, who dignify as " enterprises of great pith and
moment," the actions of those who like Fortinbras

" Make mouths at the invisible event,"

are but poorly fitted to judge of one to whom " the
invisible event" is the whole. That regard which
checked Macbeth's action in part, checked Hamlet's
altogether. We may, by and by, come to see that

there may be more of true heroic action in a mental
conflict that never results in a deed, than in a thou-
sand that do; that it is at the root of the tree of
self within the heart, that Christ has laid the axe; and
that here fall the blows that sound loudest and farth-
est through the kingdom of Satan. We have to do
with this world only, and the objects of sense which
are our daily care, unmodified by the great ideas of
death and eternity, stand before us in a light and
greatness not their own. Hamlet, on the other hand,
is dealing with both worlds at once; and, under the
influence of those spiritual realities which should
qualify *our* thoughts, he describes objects in a man-
ner, which from our position appears very strange
and distorting. Under the transforming power of
such ideas, what seems to us of permanent shape
and coloring, to him is like a many-tinted cloud
continually varying in hue and form.

Hamlet.   Do you see yonder cloud, that's almost
in the shape of a camel?

Polonius.   By the mass, and 'tis like a camel in-
deed.

Hamlet.   Methinks, it is like a weasel.

Polonius.   It is backed like a weasel.

Hamlet.   Or, like a whale?

Polonius.   Very like a whale.

After all that has been said to explain the apparent inactivity of Hamlet, we must still feel that, although we have accounted for, and shown the naturalness of his delay, yet the character of the son, and he "the son of a dear father murdered," is still somewhat less earnest in Hamlet than we should have expected. This particular view of his circumstance, which we have given, is pressed too far home to be *entirely* natural. It seems as if Shakspeare, feeling a more than common sympathy with the situation he had assumed for the expression of his own feelings, put too much of himself, so to speak, in the composition. We feel that Hamlet is rather such a son as Shakspeare would have made, than the Hamlet of the king's own household. The poet's intention in this play was not, we think, as Goethe says, " to exhibit the effects of a great action imposed as a duty on a mind too feeble for its accomplishment ;" nor, as Coleridge expresses it, " to exhibit a character flying from the sense of reality and seeking a reprieve from the pressure of its duties in that ideal activity, the overbalance of which with the consequent indisposition to action is Hamlet's disease." These are but accidents, and had the design been such as these suppose in Shakspeare, this play would never have been written. No, it was not for ends like these, but for an end of which these should prove but accidents. Was he strongly sensible of a

purpose, — it must have been to open to our view that
wild tumultuous sea of thoughts which was rolling in
the breast of Hamlet, when the idea of death and
the presence of things invisible, stood sensible to
sight and touch before him.   This thought, breaking
upon him in so terrible and unexpected a form, tore
from life, at one rude grasp, the gaudy and alluring
attire with which it is arrayed to the eye of sense ;
and, blotting out " all trivial fond records, all saws of
books," it fronted him in its own grim reality. Well
might he feel, if this was all there was of living, to
him it was valueless.   Unlike Claudio and Macbeth,
the goods of this world, were they all, appeared not
to him of consequence enough to deserve a moment's
regard ; — in the wide firmament of his vision, time
and space had dwindled to what they really are,
but golden points of an immensity.

Hamlet has been called mad, but, as we think,
Shakspeare thought more of his madness than he did
of the wisdom of the rest of the play.   Like the
vision-struck Paul, in the presence of Felix, he
spoke what to those around him, whose eyes had not
been opened on that light brighter than the sun,
seemed madness ; but which was, in fact, the words
of truth and soberness.   Men have felt that though
mad, as they thought, there was still a method in it ;
and that there was something in his language which
revealed them to themselves, and to which, though

ignorant of its full meaning, every human heart must and does beat responsive. We must not suppose from the impression that words make upon *us*, that we necessarily understand what they mean to others. We are but too apt to mistake for knowledge the sounds that give us a mere outside recognition of the states of mind from which they proceeded. It is the spirit that quickens what we hear, — the mere hearing is nothing. The words which I say to you, says our Savior, are *spirit*, and quicken with *eternal* life, — they are not addressed to the flesh, nor are they life-giving to that. We must not think, because we know the dictionary meaning of the word Death, and can enumerate a few of the sensible changes it produces, that we know its *whole* meaning, — all that one feels when it has become a frequent thought to his mind, modifying, as it was designed to do, every other thought. Much less must we suppose ourselves to have found the divine meaning of that eternal life of which Jesus speaks; until we have experienced that death of our own wills, against which we are to strive continually in our minds unto blood. Shakspeare's words too, like those of all true men, have a meaning whose fulness can only be felt by a spirit in a similar state to his from whose lips they fell. Spoken without this, they are but sounds filling the empty chambers of the soul with noisy echoes. They pass be-

fore us, dim and shadowy, as the phantom kings be-
fore the eyes of Macbeth, the silent witnesses of a
world to us unrealized;—speechless, save as the
workings of our own souls give them utterance. Let
us not then suppose, that, by treasuring up the golden
language that has fallen from other tongues of pow-
er, we are gaining for ourselves a fast possession;
for unless their spirit is growing up within us,
to fill their dumb words with the eloquence of life,
our piled wealth, like the rich colored leaves of au-
tumn, will shrink in our hands to the dark and worth-
less emblems of decay.

We need not go farther to show, what will now be
apparent, the tendency of Shakspeare to overact
this particular part of Hamlet, and thus give it an
obscurity from too close a connexion with his own
mind,—a state so difficult to approach. It is plain
that to him the thought of death, and the condition
of being to which that change might subject him,
would ever be his nearest thoughts; and that, where-
ever there exists the strong sense of life, these ideas
must follow hard upon it. In the question of Ham-
let, the *thoughts*, as well as the words, have their
natural order, when "to be" is followed by "not to
be." And we think that no one can read the words of
Claudio, or the soliloquy of Hamlet, without thinking
that, for Shakspeare, they must have had no com-
mon meaning. Here we find a reason for his occu-

pying so strongly this particular position. This idea
not only renders the inconsistencies of Hamlet har-
monious, but places also the whole tragedy on a
common ground with the rest of Shakspeare's plays.
Viewed in its light they all become but part and par-
cel of one mind ; without it, Hamlet must always re-
main, as it has hitherto done, a character apart from
that of the others, darkened with a mystery too deep
for us to scan. Our thoughts, and those of Hamlet
and Shakspeare are strangely opposite. With them,
to be or not to be, — that is the question ; with us there
is no question at all about that, — we take that to be
settled. With us, to be rich or not to be rich, to be
wise or not to be wise, to be honored or not to be
honored, — those are the questions. It is because we
live so continually in this state of mind, that we are
unable to conceive of Hamlet's character, and to see
Shakspeare himself in his creations. This it is that
inclines many to say of the celebrated soliloquy, as
Goldsmith has said, that it " is in our opinion, a heap
of absurdities, whether we consider the situation, the
sentiments, the argumentation or the poetry ; that
it does not appear that Hamlet had the least reason
to wish for death, but every motive which may be
supposed to influence, concurred to render life de-
sirable, — revenge towards the usurper ; love for the
fair Ophelia ; and the ambition of reigning." We
should naturally think with Goldsmith, and think

rightly, that if these were all the motives that influ-
enced Shakspeare in the conception of Hamlet, there
were a great many things in the play besides the so-
liloquy, that were out of place. Johnson viewed it
also in this manner, and, in consequence, says;
" that there are some scenes which neither forward
nor retard the action, and that for the feigned mad-
ness of Hamlet there is no adequate cause, for he
does nothing which he might not have done with the
reputation of sanity." But the moment we consid-
er that this is but a quarter thought by which we
would endeavour to explain the whole ; and that the
largest half of his design must have been to show
the action in which his own mind was thrown in
Hamlet's case, these difficulties at once clear up ;
and the parts that before stood out as dark and un-
sightly excrescences from the play, become, in an in-
stant, its gilded summits of light. The thoughts of
the soliloquy are not found to belong to a particular
part of this play, but to be the spirit of the whole.
To be or not to be is written over its every scene
from the entrance of the ghost, to the rude inscrip-
tion over the gate-way of the church-yard ; and,
whenever we shall have built up, in ourselves, the
true conception of this the greatest of the poets,
To be or not to be, will be found to be chiselled in
golden letters on the very key-stone of that arch
which tells us of his memory.

It is this mystery which hangs over our being, and which Shakspeare felt more strongly, perhaps, than any other of our race ever did, that enabled him to cast so deep the dark foundations of his supernatural beings, and give them all but that power over us which their actual visitation would have. It is not that the ghost has usurped the form and majesty of buried Denmark, and

> " again in complete steel
> Revisits thus the glimpses of the moon,
> Making night hideous,"

that he chains us with awe ; but it is because he has usurped a form which, in the moments when we are most ourselves, our own souls *will* summon up to question the secrets of their destiny. *We* do not fear it more than Hamlet; for we feel there is some natural connection between us and another world, " being," as he says, " things immortal as itself." And again, in the soliloquy, when Hamlet speaks of

> " The undiscovered country, from whose bourne
> No traveller returns"—

why has he forgotten his spiritual visitant, unless it was to show us how trifling and unimportant this incident was in the play, before the great reality of a soul unsatisfied in its longings after immortality ?

A state of mind like this affords an easy and nat-
ural solution of Hamlet's treatment of Ophelia. He
loved her deeply, — deeper than aught else ; yet when
she broke in upon his soliloquy, in which existence
itself now and forever seemed questionable, and
the sun, on which that world of love within his
bosom hung, seemed ready to be blotted out, the
thought of all this might well work in him that
bitterness, whose poignance but the more strongly
proved his love. The view of the world and all its
hopes and fears which he has just expressed, is a
sufficient explanation of the whole scene. As he
has said before, man delights him not nor woman
neither; and as the thought too of his uncle's and
his mother's wickedness presses upon his mind, and
there seems to him nothing that can be trusted, no-
thing sure; we may pardon the harshness of his
words to Ophelia, "Get thee to a nunnery; why
shouldst thou be a breeder of sinners?" Then too
we may sympathize with him, when, as if to palliate
a harshness which in his present state of mind he
cannot but feel, he turns with like reproach upon
himself—"I am myself indifferent honest." His
language therefore, in this scene, is in perfect keep-
ing with the rest of the play, and his own character.
There is no dissimulation, as has been supposed, —
for there was need of none.

The words of Hamlet as a lover are, as we think,

in some respects parallel to those addressed by him
as a son to his father's shade, — when he exclaims
to the ghost beneath ; " Ha, ha, boy ! sayst thou so ;
art thou there, true penny ?" and again — " Well
said, old mole ! canst work in the earth so fast ?" In
the height of emotion and mental conflict to which
he is raised by these contemplations, he finds re-
lief, as in the grave yard, in expressions which
seem strangely at variance with each other ; but
which, in reality, are but natural alternations. So
much does he dwell in the world of spirits that there
is a sort of ludicrous aspect upon which his mind
seizes as often as it returns to this. " There is
something," says Scott, " in my deepest afflictions
and most gloomy hours, that compels me to mix
with my distresses strange snatches of mirth, which
have no mirth in them."

Before we lose sight of this noblest, yet still un-
appreciated monument of Shakspeare's mind, we
cannot but pause for a moment and look back with
awe and admiration upon its dark and majestic out-
line, as it stands towering against the sky, — the
kingly pyramid of the prince of Denmark covering
in its secret chambers a mystery more hidden, and
precious, than that which the pile of an Egyptian
monarch, though reared with a thousand hands, is
fabled to conceal. His thoughts, though common
with us as the sun-light and the air, are, like them,

mighty hieroglyphics which may indeed have false
meanings attached to them, but which can never be
interpreted until the wisdom of God is shed abroad
in our hearts. Then shall we read and understand.
Then may we be touched by his own sadness as we
listen to this last farewell of our Shakspeare.

> " Our revels now are ended : these our actors,
>   As I foretold you, were all spirits, and
>   Are melted into air, into thin air :
>   And like the baseless fabric of this vision,
>   The cloud-capped towers, the gorgeous palaces,
>   The solemn temples, the great globe itself,
>   Yea all which it inherit shall dissolve ;
>   And like this unsubstantial pageant faded,
>   Leave not a rack behind : we are such stuff
>   As dreams are made of, and our little life
>   Is rounded with a sleep.   Sir I am vexed ;
>   Bear with my weakness ; my old brain is troub-
>   led.
>   Be not disturbed with my infirmity :
>   *   *   *   *   *   *   *   *   *   *
>
>   But hence retire me to my" AVON, " where
>   Every third thought shall be my grave."

POEMS.

POEMS.

TO THE HUMMING-BIRD.

I CANNOT heal thy green gold breast,
Where deep those cruel teeth have prest,
Nor bid thee raise thy ruffled crest,
    And seek thy mate,
Who sits alone within thy nest,
    Nor sees thy fate.

No more with him in summer hours
Thou'lt hum amid the leafy bowers,
Nor hover round the dewy flowers,
    To feed thy young;
Nor seek, when evening darkly lowers,
    Thy nest high hung.

No more thou'lt know a mother's care
Thy honied spoils at eve to share,
Nor teach thy tender brood to dare
  With upward spring,
Their path through fields of sunny air,
  On new fledged wing.

For thy return in vain shall wait
Thy tender young, thy fond fond mate,
Till night's last stars beam forth full late
  On their sad eyes;
Unknown, alas! thy cruel fate,
  Unheard thy cries!

EHEU! FUGACES, POSTHUME, POSTHUME,
LABUNTUR ANNI.

FLEETING years are ever bearing
   In their silent course away
All that in our pleasures sharing
   Lent to life a cheering ray.

Beauty's cheek but blooms to wither,
   Smiling hours but come to fly;
They are gone; Time's but the giver
   Of whate'er is doomed to die.

Thou may'st touch with blighting finger
   All that sense can here enjoy;
Yet within my soul shall linger
   That which thou canst not destroy.

Love's sweet voice shall there awaken
   Joys that earth cannot impart;
Joys that live when thou hast taken
   All that here can charm the heart.

As the years come gliding by me,
   Fancy's pleasing visions rise;
Beauty's cheek, ah! still I see thee,
   Still your glances, soft blue eyes!

LINES

TO A WITHERED LEAF SEEN ON A POET'S TABLE.

Poet's hand has placed thee there,
Autumn's brown and withered scroll!
Though to outward eye not fair,
Thou hast beauty for the soul,

Though no human pen has traced
On that leaf its learned lore,
Love divine the page has graced, —
What can words discover more?

Not alone dim Autumn's blast
Echoes from yon tablet sear, —
Distant music of the Past
Steals upon the poet's ear.

Voices sweet of summer hours,
Spring's soft whispers murmur by;
Feathered songs from leafy bowers
Draw his listening soul on high.

MEMORY.

Soon the waves so lightly bounding
    All forget the tempest blast;
Soon the pines so sadly sounding
    Cease to mourn the storm that's past.

Soon is hushed the voice of gladness
    Heard within the green wood's breast;
Yet come back no notes of sadness,
    No remembrance breaks its rest.

But the heart,— how fond t'will treasure
    Every note of grief and joy!
Oft come back the notes of pleasure,
    Grief's sad echoes oft annoy.

There still dwell the looks that vanish
    Swift as brightness of a dream;
Time in vain earth's smiles may banish,
    There undying still they beam.

TO THE PAINTED COLUMBINE.

BRIGHT image of the early years
When glowed my cheek as red as thou,
And life's dark throng of cares and fears
Were swift-winged shadows o'er my sunny brow!

Thou blushest from the painter's page,
Robed in the mimic tints of art;
But Nature's hand in youth's green age
With fairer hues first traced thee on my heart.

The morning's blush, she made it thine,
The morn's sweet breath, she gave it thee,
And in thy look, my Columbine!
Each fond-remembered spot she bade me see.

I see the hill's far-gazing head,
Where gay thou noddest in the gale;
I hear light-bounding footsteps tread
The grassy path that winds along the vale.

I hear the voice of woodland song
Break from each bush and well-known tree,
And on light pinions borne along,
Comes back the laugh from childhood's heart of glee.

O'er the dark rock the dashing brook,
With look of anger, leaps again,
And, hastening to each flowery nook,
Its distant voice is heard far down the glen.

Fair child of art! thy charms decay,
Touched by the withered hand of Time;
And hushed the music of that day,
When my voice mingled with the streamlet's chime;

But on my heart thy cheek of bloom
Shall live when Nature's smile has fled;
And, rich with memory's sweet perfume,
Shall o'er her grave thy tribute incense shed.

There shalt thou live and wake the glee
That echoed on thy native hill;
And when, loved flower! I think of thee,
My infant feet will seem to seek thee still.

8

TO THE FOSSIL FLOWER.

DARK fossil flower ! I see thy leaves unrolled,
With all thy lines of beauty freshly marked,
As when the eye of Morn beamed on thee first,
And thou first turn'dst to meet its welcome smile.
And sometimes in the coals' bright rain-bow hues,
I dream I see the colors of thy prime,
And for a moment robe thy form again
In splendor not its own.   Flower of the past !
Now as I look on thee, life's echoing tread
Falls noiseless on my ear ; the present dies ;
And o'er my soul the thoughts of distant time,
In silent waves, like billows from the sea,
Come roling on and on, with ceaseless flow,
Innumerable.   Thou may'st have sprung unsown
Into thy noon of life, when first earth heard
Its Maker's sovereign voice ; and laughing flowers
Waved o'er the meadows, hung on mountain crags,
And nodded in the breeze on every hill.
Thou may'st have bloomed unseen, save by the stars
That sang together o'er thy rosy birth,
And came at eve to watch thy folded rest.
None may have sought thee on thy fragrant home,
Save   light-voiced winds that round thy dwelling
            played,

Or seemed to sigh, as oft their winged haste
Compelled their feet to roam. Thou may'st have
  lived
Beneath the light of later days, when man
With feet free-roving as the homeless wind,
Scaled the thick-mantled height, coursed plains un-
  shorn,
Breaking the solitude of nature's haunt
With voice that seemed to blend, in one sweet strain,
The mingled music of the elements.
And when against his infant frame they rose,
Uncurbed, unawed by his yet feeble hand,
And when the muttering storm, and shouting wave,
And rattling thunder, mated, round him raged,
And seemed at times like dæmon foes to gird,
Thou may'st have won with gentle look his heart,
And stirred the first warm prayer of gratitude,
And been his first, his simplest altar-gift.
For thee, dark flower! the kindling sun can bring
No more the colors that it gave, nor morn,
With kindly kiss, restore thy breathing sweets :
Yet may the mind's mysterious touch recall
The bloom and fragrance of thy early prime :
For HE who to the lowly lily gave
A glory richer than to proudest king,
He painted not those darkly-shining leaves,
With blushes like the dawn, in vain ; nor gave
To thee its sweetly-scented breath, to waste

Upon the barren air.   E'en though thou stood
Alone in nature's forest-home untrod,
The first-love of the stars and sighing winds,
The mineral holds with faithful trust thy form,
To wake in human hearts sweet thoughts of love,
Now the dark past hangs round thy memory.

TO THE CANARY BIRD.

I CANNOT hear thy voicè with others' ears,
Who make of thy lost liberty a gain ;
And in thy tale of blighted hopes and fears
Feel not that every note is born with pain.
Alas ! that with thy music's gentle swell
Past days of joy should through thy memory
    throng,
And each to thee their words of sorrow tell,
While ravished sense forgets thee in thy song.
The heart that on the past and future feeds,
And pours in human words its thoughts divine,
Though at each birth the spirit inly bleéds,
Its song may charm the listening ear like thine,
And men with gilded cage and praise will try
To make the bard like thee forget his native sky.

NATURE.

NATURE! my love for thee is deeper far
Than strength of words though spirit-born can tell;
For while I gaze they seem my soul to bar,
That in thy widening streams would onward swell
Bearing thy mirrored beauty on its breast, —
Now, through thy lonely haunts unseen to glide,
A motion that scarce knows itself from rest,
With pictured flowers and branches on its tide;
Then, by the noisy city's frowning wall,
Whose armed heights within its waters gleam,
To rush with answering voice to ocean's call,
And mingle with the deep its swollen stream,
Whose boundless bosom's calm alone can hold,
That heaven of glory in thy skies unrolled.

THE TREE.

I LOVE thee when thy swelling buds appear
And one by one their tender leaves unfold,
As if they knew that warmer suns were near,
Nor longer sought to hide from winter's cold;
And when with darker growth thy leaves are seen
To veil from view the early robin's nest,
I love to lie beneath thy waving skreen
With limbs by summer's heat and toil opprest;
And when the autumn winds have stript thee bare,
And round thee lies the smooth untrodden snow,
When nought is thine that made thee once so fair,
I love to watch thy shadowy form below,
And through thy leafless arms to look above
On stars that brighter beam when most we need their
     love.

THE STRANGER'S GIFT.

I found far culled from fragrant field and grove
Each flower that makes our Spring a welcome
    guest ;
In one sweet bond of brotherhood inwove
An osier band their leafy stalks compressed ;
A stranger's hand had made their bloom my own,
And fresh their fragrance rested on the air ;
His gift was mine — but he who gave unknown,
And my heart sorrowed though the flowers were
    fair.
Now oft I grieve to meet them on the lawn,
As sweetly scattered round my path they grow,
By One who on their petals paints the dawn,
And gilt with sunset splendors bids them glow,
For I ne'er asked ' who steeps them in perfume ?'
Nor anxious sought His love who crowns them all
    with bloom.

THY BEAUTY FADES.

THY beauty fades and with it too my love,
For 'twas the self-same stalk that bore its flower;
Soft fell the rain, and breaking from above
The sun looked out upon our nuptial hour;
And I had thought forever by thy side
With bursting buds of hope in youth to dwell,
But one by one Time strewed thy petals wide,
And every hope's wan look a grief can tell:
For I had thoughtless lived beneath his sway,
Who like a tyrant dealeth with us all,
Crowning each rose, though rooted on decay,
With charms that shall the spirit's love enthral,
And for a season turn the soul's pure eyes
From virtue's changeless bloom that time and death
        defies.

BEAUTY.

I GAZED upon thy face,— and beating life
Once stilled its sleepless pulses in my breast,
And every thought whose being was a strife
Each in its silent chamber sank to rest;
I was not, save it were a thought of thee,
Thé world was but a spot where thou hadst trod,
From every star thy glance seemed fixed on me,
Almost I loved thee better than my God.
And still I gaze,— but 'tis a holier thought
Than that in which my spirit lived before,
Each star a purer ray of love has caught,
Earth wears a lovelier robe than then it wore,
And every lamp that burns around thy shrine
Is fed with fire whose fountain is Divine.

THE WIND-FLOWER.

Thou lookest up with meek confiding eye
Upon the clouded smile of April's face,
Unharmed though Winter stands uncertain by
Eyeing with jealous glance each opening grace
Thou trustest wisely! in thy faith arrayed
More glorious thou than Israel's wisest King;
Such faith was his whom men to death betrayed
As thine who hear'st the timid voice of Spring,
While other flowers still hide them from her call
Along the river's brink and meadow bare.
Thee will I seek beside the stony wall,
And in thy trust with childlike heart would share,
O'erjoyed that in thy early leaves I find
A lesson taught by him who loved all human kind.

THE ROBIN.

Thou need'st not flutter from thy half-built nest,
Whene'er thou hear'st man's hurrying feet go by,
Fearing his eye for harm may on thee rest,
Or he thy young unfinished cottage spy ;
All will not heed thee on that swinging bough,
Nor care that round thy shelter spring the leaves,
Nor watch thee on the pool's wet margin now
For clay to plaster straws thy cunning weaves ;
All will not hear thy sweet out-pouring joy,
That with morn's stillness blends the voice of song,
For over-anxious cares their souls employ,
That else upon thy music borne along
And the light wings of heart-ascending prayer
Iad learned that Heaven is pleased thy simple joys
        to share.

THE COLUMBINE.

STILL, still my eye will gaze long fixed on thee,
Till I forget that I am called a man,
And at thy side fast-rooted seem to be,
And the breeze comes my cheek with thine to fan.
Upon this craggy hill our life shall pass,
A life of summer days and summer joys,
Nodding our honey-bells mid pliant grass
In which the bee half hid his time employs;
And here we'll drink with thirsty pores the rain,
And turn dew-sprinkled to the rising sun,
And look when in the flaming west again
His orb across the heaven its path has run;
Here left in darkness on the rocky steep,
My weary eyes shall close like folding flowers in
    sleep.

THE NEW BIRTH.

'Tis a new life ; — thoughts move not as they did
With slow uncertain steps across my mind,
In thronging haste fast pressing on they bid
The portals open to the viewless wind
That comes not save when in the dust is laid
The crown of pride that gilds each mortal brow,
And from before man's vision melting fade
The heavens and earth ; — their walls are falling
    now. —
Fast crowding on, each thought asks utterance strong ;
Storm-lifted waves swift rushing to the shore,
On from the sea they send their shouts along,
Back through the cave-worn rocks their thunders
    roar ;
And I a child of God by Christ made free
Start from death's slumbers to Eternity.

THE SON.

FATHER I wait thy word.   The sun doth stand
Beneath the mingling line of night and day,
A listening servant, waiting thy command
To roll rejoicing on its silent way ;
The tongue of time abides the appointed hour,
Till on our ear its solemn warnings fall ;
The heavy cloud withholds the pelting shower,
Then every drop speeds onward at thy call ;
The bird reposes on the yielding bough,
With breast unswollen by the tide of song,
So does my spirit wait thy presence now
To pour thy praise in quickening life along,
Chiding with voice divine man's lengthened sleep,
While round the Unuttered Word and Love their
vigils keep.

IN HIM WE LIVE.

FATHER! I bless thy name that I do live,
And in each motion am made rich with thee,
That when a glance is all that I can give,
It is a kingdom's wealth if I but see;
This stately body cannot move, save I·
Will to its nobleness my little bring;
My voice its measured cadence will not try,
Save I with every note consent to sing;
I cannot raise my hands to hurt or bless,
But I with every action must conspire;
To show me there how little I possess,
And yet that little more than I desire;
  May each new act my new allegiance prove,
Till in thy perfect love I ever live and move.

ENOCH.

I LOOKED to find a man who walked with God,
Like the translated patriarch of old ; —
Though gladdened millions on his footstool trod,
Yet none with him did such sweet converse hold ;
I heard the wind in low complaint go by
That none its melodies like him could hear ;
Day unto day spoke wisdom from on high,
Yet none like David turned a willing ear ;
God walked alone unhonored through the earth ;
For him no heart-built temple open stood,
The soul forgetful of her nobler birth
Had hewn him lofty shrines of stone and wood,
And left unfinished and in ruins still
The only temple he delights to fill.

9

THE MORNING WATCH.

'TIS near the morning watch, the dim lamp burns
But scarcely shows how dark the slumbering street;
No sound of life the silent mart returns ;
No friends from house to house their neighbors
    greet ;
It is the sleep of death ; a deeper sleep
Than e'er before on mortal eyelids fell ;
No stars above the gloom their places keep ;
No faithful watchmen of the morning tell ;
Yet still they slumber on, though rising day
Hath through their windows poured the awakening
    light;
Or, turning in their sluggard trances, say —
" There yet are many hours to fill the night ;"
They rise not yet ; while on the bridegroom goes
'Till he the day's bright gates forever on them close !

THE LIVING GOD.

THERE is no death with Thee! each plant and tree
In living haste their stems push onward still,
The pointed blade, each rooted trunk we see
In various movement all attest thy will;
The vine must die when its long race is run,
The tree must fall when it no more can rise;
The worm has at its root his task begun,
And hour by hour his steady labor plies;
Nor man can pause but in thy will must grow,
And, as his roots within more deep extend,
He shall o'er sons of sons his branches throw,
And to the latest born his shadows lend;
Nor know in thee disease nor length of days,
But lift his head forever in thy praise.

THE GARDEN.

I saw the spot where our first parents dwelt;
And yet it wore to me no face of change,
For while amid its fields and groves I felt
As if I had not sinned, nor thought it strange;
My eye seemed but a part of every sight,
My ear heard music in each sound that rose,
Each sense forever found a new delight,
Such as the spirit's vision only knows;
Each act some new and ever-varying joy
Did by my father's love for me prepare;
To dress the spot my ever fresh employ,
And in the glorious whole with Him to share;
No more without the flaming gate to stray,
No more for sin's dark stain the debt of death to pay.

THE SONG.

WHEN I would sing of crooked streams and fields,
On, on from me they stretch too far and wide,
And at their look my song all powerless yields,
And down the river bears me with its tide ;
Amid the fields I am a child again,
The spots that then I loved I love the more,
My fingers drop the strangely-scrawling pen,
And I remember nought but nature's lore ;
I plunge me in the river's cooling wave,
Or on the embroidered bank admiring lean,
Now some endangered insect life to save,
Now watch the pictured flowers and grasses **green** ;
Forever playing where a boy I played,
By hill and grove, by field and stream delayed.

LOVE.

I ASKED of Time to tell me where was Love;
He pointed to her foot-steps on the snow,
Where first the angel lighted from above,
And bid me note the way and onward go;
Through populous streets of cities spreading wide,
By lonely cottage rising on the moor,
Where bursts from sundered cliff the struggling
    tide,
To where it hails the sea with answering roar,
She led me on; o'er mountains' frozen head,
Where mile on mile still stretches on the plain,
Then homeward whither first my feet she led,
I traced her path along the snow again,
But there the sun had melted from the earth
The prints where first she trod, a child of mortal
    birth.

DAY.

Day! I lament that none can hymn thy praise
In fitting strains, of all thy riches bless;
Though thousands sport them in thy golden rays,
Yet none like thee their Maker's name confess.
Great fellow of my being! woke with me
Thou dost put on thy dazzling robes of light,
And onward from the east go forth to free
Thy children from the bondage of the night;
I hail thee, pilgrim! on thy lonely way,
Whose looks on all alike benignant shine;
A child of light, like thee, I cannot stay,
But on the world I bless must soon decline,
New rising still, though setting to mankind,
And ever in the eternal West my dayspring find.

NIGHT.

I THANK thee, Father, that the night is near
When I this conscious being may resign ;
Whose only task thy words of love to hear,
And in thy acts to find each act of mine ;
A task too great to give a child like me,
The myriad-handed labors of the day,
Too many for my closing eyes to see,
Thy words too frequent for my tongue to say ;
Yet when thou see'st me burthened by thy love,
Each other gift more lovely then appears,
For dark-robed night comes hovering from above,
And all thine other gifts to me endears ;
And while within her darkened couch I sleep,
Thine eyes untired above will constant vigils keep.

THE LATTER RAIN.

THE latter rain, — it falls in anxious haste
Upon the sun-dried fields and branches bare,
Loosening with searching drops the rigid waste,
As if it would each root's lost strength repair ;
But not a blade grows green as in the Spring,
No swelling twig puts forth its thickening leaves ;
The robins only mid the harvests sing
Pecking the grain that scatters from the sheaves ;
The rain falls still, — the fruit all ripened drops,
It pierces chestnut burr and walnut shell,
The furrowed fields disclose the yellow crops,
Each bursting pod of talents used can tell,
And all that once received the early rain
Declare to man it was not sent in vain.

THE SLAVE.

I saw him forging link by link his chain,
Yet while he felt its length he thought him free,
And sighed for those borne o'er the barren main
To bondage that to his would freedom be;
Yet on he walked with eyes far-gazing still
On wrongs that from his own dark bosom flowed,
And while he thought to do his master's will
He but the more his disobedience showed;
I heard a wild rose by the stony wall,
Whose fragrance reached me in the passing gale,
A lesson give — it gave alike to all —
And I repeat the moral of its tale,
" That from the spot where deep its dark roots grew
Bloomed forth the fragrant rose that all delight to
        view."

BREAD.

Long do we live upon the husks of corn,
While 'neath untasted lie the kernels still,
Heirs of the kingdom, but in Christ unborn,
Fain with swine's food would we our hunger fill ;
We eat, but 'tis not of the bread from heaven ;
We drink, but 'tis not from the stream of life ;
Our swelling actions want the little leaven
To make them with the sighed-for blessing rife ;
We wait unhappy on a stranger's board,
While we the master's friend by right should live,
Enjoy with him the fruits our labors stored,
And to the poor with him the pittance give ;
No more to want, the long expected heir
With Christ the Father's love forevermore to share.

THE SPIRIT LAND.

FATHER! thy wonders do not singly stand,
Nor far removed where feet have seldom strayed;
Around us ever lies the enchanted land
In marvels rich to thine own sons displayed;
In finding thee are all things round us found;
In losing thee are all things lost beside;
Ears have we but in vain strange voices sound,
And to our eyes the vision is denied;
We wander in the country far remote,
Mid tombs and ruined piles in death to dwell;
Or on the records of past greatness dote,
And for a buried soul the living sell;
While on our path bewildered falls the night
That ne'er returns us to the fields of light.

WORSHIP.

THERE is no worship now, — the idol stands
Within the spirit's holy resting place!
Millions before it bend with upraised hands,
And with their gifts God's purer shrine disgrace;
The prophet walks unhonored mid the crowd
That to the idol's temple daily throng;
His voice unheard above their voices loud,
His strength too feeble 'gainst the torrent strong;
But there are bounds that ocean's rage can stay
When wave on wave leaps madly to the shore:
And soon the prophet's word shall men obey,
And hushed to peace the billows cease to roar;
For he who spoke — and warring winds kept peace,
Commands again — and man's wild passions cease.

THE SOLDIER.

He was not armed like those of eastern clime,
Whose heavy axes felled their heathen foe;
Nor was he clad like those of later time,
Whose breast-worn cross betrayed no cross below;
Nor was he of the tribe of Levi born,
Whose pompous rites proclaim how vain their prayer;
Whose chilling words are heard at night and morn,
Who rend their robes but still their hearts would
    spare;
But he nor steel nor sacred robe had on,
Yet went he forth in God's almighty power;
He spoke the word whose will is ever done
From day's first dawn till earth's remotest hour;
And mountains melted from his presence down,
And hell affrighted fled before his frown.

THE TREES OF LIFE.

For those who worship Thee there is no death,
For all they do is but with Thee to dwell;
Now while I take from Thee this passing breath,
It is but of thy glorious name to tell;
Nor words nor measured sounds have I to find,
But in them both my soul doth ever flow;
They come as viewless as the unseen wind,
And tell thy noiseless steps where'er I go;
The trees that grow along thy living stream,
And from its springs refreshment ever drink,
Forever glittering in thy morning beam
They bend them o'er the river's grassy brink
And as more high and wide their branches grow
They look more fair within the depths below.

THE SPIRIT.

I WOULD not breathe, when blows thy mighty wind
O'er desolate hill and winter-blasted plain,
But stand in waiting hope if I may find
Each flower recalled to newer life again
That now unsightly hides itself from Thee,
Amid the leaves or rustling grasses dry,
With ice-cased rock and snowy-mantled tree
Ashamed lest Thou its nakedness should spy;
But Thou shalt breathe and every rattling bough
Shall gather leaves; each rock with rivers flow;
And they that hide them from thy presence now
In new found robes along thy path shall glow,
And meadows at thy coming fall and rise,
Their green waves sprinkled with a thousand eyes.

THE PRESENCE.

I sit within my room, and joy to find
That Thou who always lov'st, art with me here,
That I am never left by Thee behind,
But by thyself Thou keep'st me ever near;
The fire burns brighter when with Thee I look,
And seems a kinder servant sent to me;
With gladder heart I read thy holy book,
Because thou art the eyes by which I see;
This aged chair, that table, watch and door
Around in ready service ever wait;
Nor can I ask of Thee a menial more
To fill the measure of my large estate,
For Thou thyself, with all a father's care,
Where'er I turn, art ever with me there.

10

THE DEAD.

I SEE them, — crowd on crowd they walk the earth
Dry leafless trees to autumn wind laid bare ;
And in their nakedness find cause for mirth,
And all unclad would winter's rudeness dare ;
No sap doth through their clattering branches flow,
Whence springing leaves and blossoms bright ap-
　　　pear ;
Their hearts the living God have ceased to know
Who gives the spring time to th' expectant year ;
They mimic life, as if from him to steal
His glow of health to paint the livid cheek ;
They borrow words for thoughts they cannot feel,
That with a seeming heart their tongue may speak ;
And in their show of life more dead they live
Than those that to the earth with many tears they
　　　give.

I WAS SICK AND IN PRISON.

Thou hast not left the rough-barked tree to grow
Without a mate upon the river's bank;
Nor dost Thou on one flower the rain bestow,
But many a cup the glittering drops has drank;
The bird must sing to one who sings again,
Else would her note less welcome be to hear;
Nor hast Thou bid thy word descend in vain,
But soon some answering voice shall reach my ear;
Then shall the brotherhood of peace begin,
And the new song be raised that never dies,
That shall the soul from death and darkness win,
And burst the prison where the captive lies;
And one by one new-born shall join the strain,
Till earth restores her sons to heaven again.

THE VIOLET.

Thou tellest truths unspoken yet by man
By this thy lonely home and modest look;
For he has not the eyes such truths to scan,
Nor learns to read from such a lowly book;
With him it is not life firm-fixed to grow
Beneath the outspreading oaks and rising pines,
Content this humble lot of thine to know,
The nearest neighbor of the creeping vines;
Without fixed root he cannot trust like thee
The rain will know the appointed hour to fall,
But fears lest sun or shower may hurtful be,
And would delay or speed them with his call;
Nor trust like thee when wintry winds blow cold,
Whose shrinking form the withered leaves enfold.

THE HEART.

THERE is a cup of sweet or bitter drink,
Whose waters ever o'er the brim must well,
Whence flow pure thoughts of love as angels
        think,
Or of its dæmon depths the tongue will tell;
That cup can ne'er be cleansed from outward stains
While from within the tide forever flows;
And soon it wearies out the fruitless pains
The treacherous hand on such a task bestows;
But ever bright its chrystal sides appear,
While runs the current from its outlet pure;
And pilgrims hail its sparkling waters near,
And stoop to drink the healing fountain sure,
And bless the cup that cheers their fainting soul
While through this parching waste they seek their
        heavenly goal.

THE ROBE.

Each naked branch, the yellow leaf or brown,
The rugged rock, and death-deformed plain
Lie white beneath the winter's feathery down,
Nor doth a spot unsightly now remain;
On sheltering roof, on man himself it falls;
But him no robe, not spotless snow makes clean;
Beneath, his corse-like spirit ever calls,
That on it too may fall the heavenly screen;
But all in vain, its guilt can never hide
From the quick spirit's heart-deep searching eye,
There barren plains, and caverns yawning wide
Ever lie naked to the passer by;
Nor can one thought deformed the presence shun,
But to the spirit's gaze stands bright as in the sun.

LIFE.

It is not life upon Thy gifts to live,
But, to grow fixed with deeper roots in Thee;
And when the sun and shower their bounties give,
To send out thick-leaved limbs; a fruitful tree,
Whose green head meets the eye for many a mile,
Whose moss-grown arms their rigid branches rear,
And full-faced fruits their blushing welcome smile
As to its goodly shade our feet draw near;
Who tastes its gifts shall never hunger more,
For 'tis the Father spreads the pure repast,
Who, while we eat, renews the ready store,
Which at his bounteous board must ever last;
For none the bridegroom's supper shall attend,
Who will not hear and make his word their friend.

THE WAR.

I saw a war, yet none the trumpet blew,
Nor in their hands the steel-wrought weapons bare ;
And in that conflict armed there fought but few,
And none that in the world's loud tumults share ;
They fought against their wills, — the stubborn foe
That mail-clad warriors left unfought within,
And wordy champions left unslain below, —
The ravening wolf though drest in fleecy skin ; —
They fought for peace, — not that the world can give,
Whose tongue proclaims the war its hands have
          ceased
And bids us as each other's neighbor live,
Ere haughty Self within us has deceased ;
They fought for him whose kingdom must increase,
Good will to men, on earth forever peace.

THE GRAVE YARD.

My heart grows sick before the wide-spread death,
That walks and speaks in seeming life around ;
And I would love the corse without a breath,
That sleeps forgotten 'neath the cold, cold ground ;
For these do tell the story of decay,
The worm and rotten flesh hide not nor lie ;
But this, though dying too from day to day,
With a false show doth cheat the longing eye ;
And hide the worm that gnaws the core of life,
With painted cheek and smooth deceitful skin ;
Covering a grave with sights of darkness rife,
A secret cavern filled with death and sin ;
And men walk o'er these graves and know it not,
For in the body's health the soul's forgot.

THY BROTHER'S BLOOD.

I HAVE no Brother, — they who meet me now
Offer a hand with their own wills defiled,
And, while they wear a smooth unwrinkled brow,
Know not that Truth can never be beguiled ;
Go wash the hand that still betrays thy guilt ;—
Before the spirit's gaze what stain can hide ?
Abel's red blood upon the earth is spilt,
And by thy tongue it cannot be denied ;
I hear not with the ear, — the heart doth tell
Its secret deeds to me untold before ;
Go, all its hidden plunder quickly sell,
Then shalt thou cleanse thee from thy brother's
       gore,
Then will I take thy gift ; — that bloody stain
Shall not be seen upon thy hand again.

THE JEW.

THOU art more deadly than the Jew of old,
Thou hast his weapons hidden in thy speech;
And though thy hand from me thou dost withhold,
They pierce where sword and spear could never
 reach.
Thou hast me fenced about with thorny talk,
To pierce my soul with anguish while I hear;
And while amid thy populous streets I walk,
I feel at every step the entering spear;
Go, cleanse thy lying mouth of all its guile
That from the will within thee ever flows;
Go, cleanse the temple thou dost now defile,
Then shall I cease to feel thy heavy blows;
And come and tread with me the path of peace,
And from thy brother's harm forever cease.

FAITH.

THERE is no faith; the mountain stands within
Still unrebuked, its summit reaches heaven;
And every action adds its load of sin,
For every action wants the little leaven;
There is no prayer; it is but empty sound,
That stirs with frequent breath the yielding air,
With every pulse they are more strongly bound,
Who make the blood of goats the voice of prayer;
Oh heal them, heal them, Father, with thy word, —
Their sins cry out to thee from every side;
From son and sire, from slave and master heard,
Their voices fill the desert country wide;
And bid thee hasten to relieve and save,
By him who rose triumphant o'er the grave.

THE ARK.

THERE is no change of time and place with Thee;
Where'er I go, with me 'tis still the same;
Within thy presence I rejoice to be,
And always hallow thy most holy name;
The world doth ever change; there is no peace
Among the shallows of its storm-vexed breast;
With every breath the frothy waves increase,
They toss up mire and dirt, they cannot rest;
I thank Thee that within thy strong-built ark
My soul across the uncertain sea can sail,
And though the night of death be long and dark,
My hopes in Christ shall reach within the veil;
And to the promised haven steady steer,
Whose rest to those who love is ever near.

THE EARTH.

I WOULD lie low, the ground on which men tread,
Swept by Thy spirit like the wind of heaven;
An earth where gushing springs and corn for bread,
By me at every season should be given;
Yet not the water or the bread that now
Supplies their tables with its daily food,
But thou wouldst give me fruit for every bough,
Such as Thou givest me, and call'st it good;
And water from the stream of life should flow,
By every dwelling that thy love has built,
Whose taste the ransomed of thy Son shall know,
Whose robes are washed from every stain of guilt;
And men would own it was thy hand that blest,
And from my bosom find a surer rest.

THE ROSE.

THE rose thou show'st me has lost all its hue,
For thou dost seem to me than it less fair;
For when I look I turn from it to you,
And feel the flower has been thine only care;
Thou could'st have grown as freely by its side
As spring these buds from out the parent stem,
But thou art from thy Father severed wide,
And turnest from thyself to look at them,
Thy words do not perfume the summer air,
Nor draw the eye and ear like this thy flower;
No bees shall make thy lips their daily care,
And sip the sweets distilled from hour to hour;
Nor shall new plants from out thy scattered seed,
O'er many a field the eye with beauty feed.

MORNING.

THE light will never open sightless eyes,
It comes to those who willingly would see ;
And every object, — hill, and stream, and skies, —
Rejoice within th' encircling line to be ;
'Tis day, — the field is filled with busy hands,
The shop resounds with noisy workmen's din,
The traveller with his staff already stands
His yet unmeasured journey to begin ;
The light breaks gently too within the breast, —
Yet there no eye awaits the crimson morn,
The forge and noisy anvil are at rest,
Nor men nor oxen tread the fields of corn,
Nor pilgrim lifts his staff, — it is no day
To those who find on earth their place to stay.

NATURE.

The bubbling brook doth leap when I come by,
Because my feet find measure with its call,
The birds know when the friend they love is nigh,
For I am known to them both great and small;
The flower that on the lovely hill-side grows
Expects me there when Spring its bloom has given;
And many a tree and bush my wanderings knows,
And e'en the clouds and silent stars of heaven;
For he who with his Maker walks aright,
Shall be their lord as Adam was before;
His ear shall catch each sound with new delight.
Each object wear the dress that then it wore;
And he, as when erect in soul he stood,
Hear from his Father's lips that all is good.

11

CHANGE.

FATHER! there is no change to live with Thee,
Save that in Christ I grow from day to day,
In each new word I hear, each thing I see,
I but rejoicing hasten on the way;
The morning comes with blushes overspread,
And I new-wakened find a morn within;
And in its modest dawn around me shed,
Thou hear'st the prayer and the ascending hymn;
Hour follows hour, the lengthening shades descend,
Yet they could never reach as far as me,
Did not thy love thy kind protection lend,
That I a child might sleep awhile on Thee,
Till to the light restored by gentle sleep
With new-found zeal I might thy precepts keep.

THE POOR.

I WALK the streets and though not meanly drest,
Yet none so poor as can with me compare;
For none though weary call me into rest,
And though I hunger, none their substance share;
I ask not for my stay the broken reed,
That fails when most I want a friendly arm;
I cannot on the loaves and fishes feed
That want the blessing that they may not harm;
I only ask the living word to hear
From tongues that now but speak to utter death;
I thirst for one cool cup of water clear
But drink the riled stream of lying breath;
And wander on though in my Fatherland,
Yet hear no welcome voice and see no beckoning
    hand.

THE CLAY.

Thou shalt do what Thou wilt with thine own hand,
Thou form'st the spirit like the moulded clay ;
For those who love Thee keep thy just command,
And in thine image grow as they obey ;
New tints and forms with every hour they take
Whose life is fashioned by thy spirit's power ;
The crimson dawn is round them when they wake,
And golden triumphs wait the evening hour ;
The queenly-sceptred night their souls receives,
And spreads their pillows 'neath her sable tent ;
Above them Sleep their palm with poppy weaves,
Sweet rest Thou hast to all who labor lent ;
That they may rise refreshed to light again
And with Thee gather in the whitening grain.

WHO HATH EARS TO HEAR LET HIM HEAR.

THE sun doth not the hidden place reveal,
Whence pours at morn his golden flood of light ;
But what the night's dark breast would fain conceal,
In its true colors walks before our sight ;
The bird does not betray the secret springs,
Whence note on note her music sweetly pours ;
Yet turns the ear attentive while she sings,
The willing heart while falls the strain adores ;
So shall the spirit tell not whence its birth,
But in its light thine untold deeds lay bare ;
And while it walks with thee flesh-clothed the earth,
Its words shall of the Father's love declare ;
And happy those whose ears shall hail its voice,
And clean within the day it gives rejoice.

TO THE PURE ALL THINGS ARE PURE.

THE flowers I pass have eyes that look at me,
The birds have ears that hear my spirit's voice,
And I am glad the leaping brook to see,
Because it does at my light step rejoice.
Come, brothers, all who tread the grassy hill,
Or wander thoughtless o'er the blooming fields,
Come learn the sweet obedience of the will ;
Thence every sight and sound new pleasure yields.
Nature shall seem another house of thine,
When he who formed thee, bids it live and play,
And in thy rambles e'en the creeping vine
Shall keep with thee a jocund holiday,
And every plant, and bird, and insect, be
Thine own companions born for harmony.

HE WAS ACQUAINTED WITH GRIEF.

I CANNOT tell the sorrows that I feel
By the night's darkness, by the prison's gloom;
There is no sight that can the death reveal
The spirit suffers in a living tomb;
There is no sound of grief that mourners raise,
No moaning of the wind, or dirge-like sea,
Nor hymns, though prophet tones inspire the lays,
That can the spirit's grief awake in thee.
Thou too must suffer as it suffers here
The death in Christ to know the Father's love;
Then in the strains that angels love to hear
Thou too shalt hear the Spirit's song above,
And learn in grief what these can never tell,
A note too deep for earthly voice to swell.

YE GAVE ME NO MEAT.

My brother, I am hungry, — give me food
Such as my Father gives me at his board ;
He has for many years been to thee good,
Thou canst a morsel then to me afford ;
I do not ask of thee a grain of that
Thou offerest when I call on thee for bread ;
This is not of the wine nor olive fat,
But those who eat of this like thee are dead ;
I ask the love the Father has for thee,
That thou should'st give it back to me again ;
This shall my soul from pangs of hunger free,
And on my parched spirit fall like rain ;
Then thou wilt prove a brother to my need,
For in the cross of Christ thou too canst bleed.

THE ACORN.

THE seed has started, — who can stay it? see,
The leaves are sprouting high above the ground;
Already o'er the flowers, its head; the tree
That rose beside it and that on it frowned,
Behold! is but a small bush by its side.
Still on! it cannot stop; its branches spread;
It looks o'er all the earth in giant pride.
The nations find upon its limbs their bread,
Its boughs their millions shelter from the heat,
Beneath its shade see kindreds, tongues, and all
That the wide world contains, they all retreat
Beneath the shelter of that acorn small
That late thou flung away; 'twas the best gift
That heaven e'er gave; — its head the low shall lift.

THE RAIL ROAD.

Thou great proclaimer to the outward eye
Of what the spirit too would seek to tell,
Onward thou go'st, appointed from on high
The other warnings of the Lord to swell;
Thou art the voice of one that through the world
Proclaims in startling tones, " Prepare the way;"
The lofty mountain from its seat is hurled,
The flinty rocks thine onward march obey;
The valleys lifted from their lowly bed
O'ertop the hills that on them frowned before,
Thou passest where the living seldom tread,
Through forests dark, where tides beneath thee roar,
And bid'st man's dwelling from thy track remove,
And would with warning voice his crooked paths
          reprove.

THE DISCIPLE.

Thou wilt my hands employ, though others find
No work for those who praise thy name aright;
And in their worldly wisdom call them blind,
Whom thou has blest with thine own spirit's sight.
But while they find no work for thee to do,
And blindly on themselves alone rely;
The child must suffer what thou sufferest too
And learn from him thou sent e'en so to die;
Thou art my Father, thou wilt give me aid
To bear the wrong the Spirit suffers here;
Thou hast thy help upon the mighty laid,
In him I trust, nor know to want or fear,
But ever onward walk secure from sin,
For he has conquered every foe within.

TIME.

THERE is no moment but whose flight doth bring
Bright clouds and fluttering leaves to deck my
        bower ;
And I within like some sweet bird must sing
To tell the story of the passing hour ;
For time has secrets that no bird has sung,
Nor changing leaf with changing season told ;
They wait the utterance of some nobler tongue
Like that which spoke in prophet tones of old ;
Then day and night, and month and year shall tell
The tale that speaks but faint from bird and bough ;
In spirit-songs their praise shall upward swell
Nor longer pass heaven's gate unheard as now,
But cause e'en angels' ears to catch the strain,
And send it back to earth in joy again.

THE CALL.

WHY art thou not awake, my son ?
The morning breaks I formed for thee ;
And I thus early by thee stand,
Thy new-awakening life to see.

Why art thou not awake, my son ?
The birds upon the bough rejoice ;
And I thus early by thee stand,
To hear with theirs thy tuneful voice.

Why sleep'st thou still ? the laborers all
Are in my vineyard ; — hear them toil,
As for the poor with harvest song,
They treasure up the wine and oil.

I come to wake thee ; haste, arise,
Or thou no share with me can find ;
Thy sandals seize, gird on thy clothes,
Or I must leave thee here behind.

THE COTTAGE.

THE house my earthly parent left
My heavenly parent still throws down,
For 'tis of air and sun bereft,
Nor stars its roof with beauty crown.

He gave it me, yet gave it not
As one whose gifts are wise and good;
'Twas but a poor and clay-built cot,
And for a time the storms withstood.

But lengthening years and frequent rain
O'ercame its strength; it tottered, fell,
And left me homeless here again,
And where to go I could not tell.

But soon the light and open air
Received me as a wandering child,
And I soon thought their house more fair,
And all my grief their love beguiled.

Mine was the grove, the pleasant field
Where dwelt the flowers I daily trod;
And there beside them too I kneeled
And called their friend my friend and God.

THE PRAYER.

WILT Thou not visit me?
The plant beside me feels thy gentle dew;
   And every blade of grass I see,
From thy deep earth its moisture drew.

  'Wilt Thou not visit me?
Thy morning calls on me with cheering tone;
   And every hill and tree
Lend but one voice, the voice of Thee alone.

  Come, for I need thy love,
More than the flower the dew, or grass the rain;
   Come, gently as thy holy dove;
And let me in thy sight rejoice to live again.

  I will not hide from them,
When thy storms come, though fierce may be their
      wrath;
   But bow with leafy stem,
And strengthened follow on thy chosen path.

  Yes, Thou wilt visit me;
Nor plant nor tree thy eye delight so well,
   As when from sin set free
My spirit loves with thine in peace to dwell.

The Romantic Tradition in American Literature

An Arno Press Collection

Alcott, A. Bronson, editor. **Conversations with Children on the Gospels.** Boston, 1836/1837. Two volumes in one.

Bartol, C[yrus] A. **Discourses on the Christian Spirit and Life.** 2nd edition. Boston, 1850.

Boker, George H[enry]. **Poems of the War.** Boston, 1864.

Brooks, Charles T. **Poems, Original and Translated.** Selected and edited by W. P. Andrews. Boston, 1885.

Brownell, Henry Howard. **War-Lyrics** and Other Poems. Boston, 1866.

Brownson, O[restes] A. **Essays and Reviews Chiefly on Theology, Politics, and Socialism.** New York, 1852.

Channing, [William] Ellery (The Younger). **Poems.** Boston, 1843.

Channing, [William] Ellery (The Younger). **Poems of Sixty-Five Years.** Edited by F. B. Sanborn. Philadelphia and Concord, 1902.

Chivers, Thomas Holley. **Eonchs of Ruby:** A Gift of Love. New York, 1851.

Chivers, Thomas Holley. **Virginalia;** or, Songs of My Summer Nights. (Reprinted from *Research Classics*, No. 2, 1942). Philadelphia, 1853.

Cooke, Philip Pendleton. **Froissart Ballads,** and Other Poems. Philadelphia, 1847.

Cranch, Christopher Pearse. **The Bird and the Bell,** with Other Poems. Boston, 1875.

[Dall], Caroline W. Healey, editor. **Margaret and Her Friends.** Boston, 1895.

[D'Arusmont], Frances Wright. **A Few Days in Athens.** Boston, 1850.

Everett, Edward. **Orations and Speeches,** on Various Occasions. Boston, 1836.

Holland, J[osiah] G[ilbert]. **The Marble Prophecy,** and Other Poems. New York, 1872.

Huntington, William Reed. **Sonnets and a Dream.** Jamaica, N. Y., 1899.

Jackson, Helen [Hunt]. **Poems.** Boston, 1892.

Miller, Joaquin (Cincinnatus Hiner Miller). **The Complete Poetical Works of Joaquin Miller.** San Francisco, 1897.

Parker, Theodore. **A Discourse of Matters Pertaining to Religion.** Boston, 1842.

Pinkney, Edward C. **Poems.** Baltimore, 1838.

Reed, Sampson. **Observations on the Growth of the Mind.** *Including,* **Genius** (Reprinted from *Aesthetic Papers,* Boston, 1849). 5th edition. Boston, 1859.

Sill, Edward Rowland. **The Poetical Works of Edward Rowland Sill.** Boston and New York, 1906.

Simms, William Gilmore. **Poems:** Descriptive, Dramatic, Legendary and Contemplative. New York, 1853. Two volumes in one.

Simms, William Gilmore, editor. **War Poetry of the South.** New York, 1866.

Stickney, Trumbull. **The Poems of Trumbull Stickney.** Boston and New York, 1905.

Timrod, Henry. **The Poems of Henry Timrod.** Edited by Paul H. Hayne. New York, 1873.

Trowbridge, John Townsend. **The Poetical Works of John Townsend Trowbridge.** Boston and New York, 1903.

Very, Jones. **Essays and Poems.** [Edited by R. W. Emerson]. Boston, 1839.

Very, Jones. **Poems and Essays.** Boston and New York, 1886.

White, Richard Grant, editor. **Poetry:** Lyrical, Narrative, and Satirical of the Civil War. New York, 1866.

Wilde, Richard Henry. **Hesperia:** A Poem. Edited by His Son (William Wilde). Boston, 1867.

Willis, Nathaniel Parker. **The Poems, Sacred, Passionate, and Humorous, of Nathaniel Parker Willis.** New York, 1868.